Favorite foreign birds for cages and aviaries

W T. Greene

Favourite Foreign Birds

and

Cages and Aviaries.

PARROTS.

PARROTS. PARROTS.

Any person wishing to Purchase one of these, the most interesting of all Birds, should send to the

Fountain Head.

Always the largest collection in Europe.

FAVOURITE
FOREIGN BIRDS

FOR

CAGES AND AVIARIES.

BY

W. T. GREENE, M.D., M.A., &c.,

Author of "Parrots in Captivity," "Birds I have Kept," "The Birds in my Garden," "Song Birds of Great Britain," "The Amateur's Aviary," "Diseases of Cage Birds," &c.; Editor of "Notes on Cage Birds."

———————

LONDON:
L. UPCOTT GILL, 170, STRAND, W.C.

LONDON :
A. BRADLEY LONDON AND COUNTY PRINTING WORKS,
DRURY LANE, W.C.

PREFACE.

OREIGN bird keeping is a very delightful pursuit, but in order to attain complete success in it, there are a few points that must be observed. For instance, the habits of the different little captives must be studied, and their food and lodgment, as well as the temperature at which they are kept, must be approximated as nearly as possible to what they were accustomed to in their own country; but it is only experience, gathered from reliable guide-books or bought by painful disaster and loss, that will enable the fancier to select those birds best suited for his circumstances, and give him the knowledge necessary for their preservation and well-being, and also for his own satisfaction.

I have borne all this in view in the following pages, and while describing the different species that experience has shown to be the most suitable subjects for domestication, have indicated the food and treatment necessary for each, and any points connected with their management that have seemed to me likely to be of use.

With these general remarks I will now refer my readers to the work itself, in the hope that the information there given will enable them to keep foreign birds not only for pleasure, but for profit; and in this connection I will observe that a well-conducted aviary should certainly be self-supporting—in some cases I have known it "pay."

W. T. GREENE.

MOIRA HOUSE,
PECKHAM RYE, SURREY.
May, 1891.

CONTENTS.

FAVOURITE FOREIGN BIRDS.

CHAPTER I.

INTRODUCTION.

Popularity of Aviculture—Native and Exotic Races Compared—Classification—Scientific Names.

AVICULTURE, long since carried to perfection in France and Germany, is yet in its infancy in Great Britain, though vastly more people are interesting themselves about birds at the present day than used to be the case a dozen years ago, when very few amateurs had any knowledge of the beautiful and attractive feathered denizens of foreign lands, many of which are now being naturalised in our midst, and have become almost as abundant as our own canaries or sparrows.

At first sight this no doubt appears extraordinary, especially when we contrast our own bleak and changeable climate with that enjoyed by the fertile and fragrant lands of which most of the foreign birds we meet with over here are natives. What a contrast, for instance, between the orange groves of Florida, or the palm-covered slopes of Western Africa, and our own country, where vegetation is dormant for half the year, and the trees are so many leafless skeletons from November to March or April! What a contrast, too, between the warmth of the same regions and the cold, damp, and fog of our native isles! So great, indeed, that one is compelled to wonder how birds indigenous to the former can ever be sufficiently acclimatised to live, and even to thrive, in the latter. Yet such is the case, and in the following pages I propose passing in review some of the different species of exotic birds which I have found adapt themselves most readily to their new surroundings in confinement.

The passion for bird-keeping—which, by the way, is steadily on the increase among us—usually has its origin in very humble beginnings; but it rapidly gains strength, and before long experiments are made and investments ventured on that, without preparation, would at one time have filled the soul of the adventurous aviarist with apprehension and awe.

Some writer has called the birds "the fairest of all God's creatures," and I think he is not far wrong. But, much as I admire our own native races, I must confess to a preference for the birds that are brought to us from foreign parts. True, the latter have not, as a rule, such musical talents as our own; but, from whatever cause, they adapt themselves much more readily to a life in confinement, in which they never, unless out of health, wear that look of sullen discontent that is characteristic of so many English cage-birds. Then also, as a rule, the foreign species are much more conspicuous for brilliancy of colouring, and even for elegance of form, than the birds that adorn our fields and hedgerows, or hide themselves as much as possible from human observation in our woods and plantations So, without entirely deprecating the keeping of native birds in confinement, I am decidedly of opinion that the acclimatisation of foreign species will be, on the whole, a greater source of gratification to the aviarist; and in the end he will also find that his hobby will cost him less than if he "went in" for keeping a collection of our British birds.

A word more, before I close these introductory remarks, as to the system, or rather want of system, that will necessarily characterise these pages. Scientific classification is out of the question where only a selection of species is reviewed; therefore I have determined to take the various groups in alphabetical order—which will, perhaps, be as convenient a method for those who may read these pages as any that I could adopt.

The scientific names given are in nearly all cases those used by the Zoological Society of London in their list of vertebrated animals, although I do not in every instance agree with its absolute correctness, and, in the matter of classification, differ with the Society in many instances.

As prices vary so much according to circumstances, it has not been thought desirable to quote any in the following pages.

CHAPTER II.

THE CARDINAL FAMILY
(*Cardinalidæ*).

The Red-crested Cardinal—The Pope, or Crestless Cardinal—The Yellow-billed Cardinal—The Black-crested Cardinal—The Cardinal Grossbeak, or Virginian Nightingale.

N this group I propose to include five species which are of frequent occurrence as cage-birds in this country : they are all natives of Brazil or the adjacent countries of Southern America, and can be readily acclimatised so as to pass the winter without injury to their constitutions in a garden aviary, where not infrequently they will be found to nest and rear their young.

The proper diet for these birds in confinement is canary- and millet-seed, grain-food of all kinds, ants' eggs, insects of every description, especially caterpillars, and all kinds of ripe fruit when in season : they appear to be especially fond of raspberries and strawberries. Hemp-seed should never be allowed, as it darkens the plumage and changes the beautiful white breasts of the three first species described to a dingy blackish-grey.

The young require a large amount of food, and after the first few days are very clamorous while being fed. I found cockroaches, commonly known as blackbeetles, a very convenient insect, and all the young Cardinals I have had were reared on no other diet.

FIG. I. THE RED-CRESTED CARDINAL.

THE RED-CRESTED CARDINAL, *Paroaria cucullata* (illustrated at Fig. 1), is a handsome, bold-looking bird, of a delicate ashen-grey colour on the back, tail, and wings; his face, chin, head, and upstanding crest are red; a collar round his neck, and all his under-parts, are pure white; his beak light horn-colour, and his legs and feet leaden-grey. He is about the size of a plump skylark, but a bolder-looking and more upstanding bird, and has a very passable song, which he is fond of rehearsing pretty well all the year round. The sexes are exactly alike in appearance, but the female may be known by her somewhat smaller size and less exuberantly boisterous deportment.

As these birds are extremely pugnacious during the breeding season, they should not be lodged with others smaller and more defenceless than themselves. The nest is built of hay, fibres, and roots, in any convenient bush; and the eggs, which vary from three to five in number, are small for the size of the bird, and not unlike those of a blackbird in colour and markings. The young can be readily reared on ants' eggs and cockroaches, or any kind of insects available. Occasionally the male evinces cannibalistic tendencies —sometimes with regard to the eggs, which he will devour as soon as laid, and sometimes with respect to newly-hatched young, which he will destroy. In such a case he should be removed after the first egg has been laid, when the female will sit and rear her brood alone—the remaining eggs of the batch proving, as a rule, to be fertile. Incubation lasts from eleven to twelve days, and there are generally two broods in the season—the first in May or June; the second in August. In their native country, of course, the seasons are reversed; but the birds readily accommodate themselves to their altered circumstances.

I have found them to be extremely destructive to plants of all kinds. Some of their eggs which I have placed under canaries, were duly hatched; but the young died in a few days, apparently from inability on the part of their foster-parents to feed them properly; but no doubt if the eggs were placed in the nest of a thrush or blackbird the young Cardinals would be reared without any difficulty, and might then be permitted to escape, when, no doubt, they would soon become acclimatised and able to shift for themselves.

THE POPE, or CRESTLESS CARDINAL, *Paroaria larvata*, is somewhat smaller than the last-named species, which it closely resembles in its plumage, the great point of difference being the total absence of a crest in the case of the bird now under consideration : it is a native of Brazil, perfectly hardy if turned out during the summer, and no more to be trusted with other, and especially smaller, species than its larger relative with the crest. Like the latter, the Popes have bred in confinement; that is to say, in the comparative freedom of a garden aviary, for I have no knowledge of their nesting in a cage, or even in a bird-room, and from their shy and retiring habits think it is extremely unlikely that they would do so.

The sexes are alike in appearance, but the female is a trifle smaller than her mate, and has a more subdued and quieter manner than he has. The eggs resemble those of the Red-crested Cardinal, but are smaller: there are two broods in the season, of from three to five each.

THE YELLOW-BILLED CARDINAL, *Paroaria capitata*, is also a native of South America, and is crestless; it is smaller than the Pope, from which it differs not only by the colour of its beak, but also in that of the head feathers, which are brownish-red, small, and very closely set. The sexes are alike, but several females I have seen showed a trace of white on the wings.

This species would appear to be more delicate than either of the preceding, and to be more insectivorous in their habits. Some I at one time possessed appeared to suffer so much from the cold of their first winter in this country—to which their hardier companions seemed perfectly indifferent—that I was forced to take them indoors. They made a nest, but did not lay; so I have no personal knowledge of their eggs, which are said, however, to closely resemble those of their congeners.

I found them quiet and uninterfering with other birds, and the song of the male was very pretty; so that, on the whole, I can cordially recommend them to the notice of amateurs.

THE BLACK-CRESTED CARDINAL, *Gubernatrix cristatella*, is very generally known, especially by dealers, as the Green Cardinal, though upon close examination it will be found that it bears no trace of green in its plumage, which is coloured black and yellow; the crest is large, jet black, and very upright, and the bird itself about the size of a thrush, but owing to its crest, and longer wings and tail, it seems larger.

Like the rest of the Cardinals, this bird comes from South America, and is quite hardy. At the Zoological Gardens in Regent's Park it has bred on several occasions, and also in the aviaries of several amateurs, but not in mine. The female is readily distinguished by her duller-coloured plumage, as well as by the size of her crest, which is not nearly as conspicuous as that of her mate.

At the "Zoo," this bird is separated from the rest of the family and placed in a genus by itself—

the genus *Gubernatrix*, of which it forms the sole representative: as well as the three preceding species, which constitute the genus *Paroaria*, it is placed in the family *Fringillidæ*—but erroneously so, I think, seeing that the Cardinals are, all of them, as much insectivorous in their choice of food as granivorous, or perhaps more so, and feed their young entirely on insects of all kinds.

FIG. 2. THE VIRGINIAN NIGHTINGALE.

THE CARDINAL GROSSBEAK, or VIRGINIAN NIGHT-INGALE, *Cardinalis virginianus* (illustrated at Fig. 2), is a handsome bird, about the size of a thrush, that is very frequently imported from the southern parts of North America; like the rest of the members of the family to which it belongs, it will eat seed, fruit, and insects, but if kept on an exclusively granivorous diet it is frequently unable to reproduce its feathers—in which case it generally dies of atrophy or decline.

As the name implies, the general colour is scarlet—
even the beak and legs partaking of the same ruddy
hue—but the throat is black. The female is of a
reddish-brown colour, and can at a glance be distinguished from her mate, who sings very sweetly,
but, in my judgment, has no pretension to be called
a nightingale.

These birds will occasionally breed in this country,
but do so less freely than their grey or green
relations; those I have had from time to time have
not made any attempt in that direction, but other
fanciers have been more fortunate. The eggs are
said to be bluish-white, speckled with olive, green,
and brown spots. The young resemble their mother,
and have a dark brown, nearly black, bill. The
treatment and feeding should be the same as for the
rest of the Cardinals.

CHAPTER III.

THE CROW FAMILY
(Corvidæ).

The White-backed Piping Crow—The Hunting Crow —The Wandering Pie—The Chinese Blue Pie— The Chinese Blue Magpie—The Spanish Blue Magpie—The Blue-bearded Jay—The Pileated Jay.

THERE are quite a number of most delightful foreign birds belonging to the Crow family, many of which make the most charming pets and should have a place in every collection: the only drawback to keeping them is that, as a rule, they are of a tyrannical disposition, and cannot be kept at close quarters with birds belonging to other families, particularly if smaller than themselves.

They may be generally described as omnivorous in their habits, and in confinement should be fed on meat, fruit, boiled maize or other corn, ants' eggs, and insects of all kinds; the two latter items for the smaller members of the family, while the larger every now and then will need a mouse or a small bird to

keep them in health. I propose taking the latter
first, premising that they are all most intelligent birds
and susceptible of being completely tamed.

THE WHITE-BACKED PIPING CROW, *Gymnorhina
leuconota,* is an Australian species, and is a general
favourite with the Colonists, by whom it is popularly
known as the Magpie, not only on account of its
susceptibility for domestication, but of the invaluable
services it renders to them by the destruction of
innumerable hosts of noxious insects, especially scorpions and monstrous centipedes, which are only a
shade less venomous than the former repulsive-looking
creatures.

This species is stated in the list of the Zoological
Society to be a native of South Australia, but this is
too restricted a habitat, as it is common in Victoria
and New South Wales, and differs but slightly from
the Tasmanian Piping Crow, of which the same
authority has constituted a distinct species under the
name of *Gymnorhina organica.*

The White-backed Piping Crow is well described
by its English name: it is a fine bird about the size
of our Carrion Crow, with a strong beak of a bluish
colour, white back, and black body.

Some of these birds, especially if reared by hand
from the nest, make most accomplished talkers, and
will also learn to whistle a tune or tunes, when, as
their voice is naturally harmonious and mellow, a very
fine effect is produced: the only drawback is that their
notes are rather too loud for the house; they are
very attractive, however, in the open air.

All the Piping Crows are quite hardy, and will winter

readily out of doors in this country; but no instance of their having nested in confinement has ever come to my knowledge, though in a suitable place I see no reason why they should not do so.

In the matter of diet they are very accommodating, and have a special predilection for picking a bone: all is fish that comes to their net, and the aviarist will not have much difficulty in providing for their wants, as they will thrive on any kind of scraps from their owner's table.

If lodged in a cage, this must be of considerable dimensions and be carefully attended to, for otherwise the Piping Crow, on account of its size and the miscellaneous nature of its diet, would soon render uninhabitable the place where it was kept. In a large outdoor aviary, however, there would not be the same objection, and, everything considered, that is the best position for such a bird, or it may be allowed the free range of a garden if one of its wings is clipped.

The female does not greatly differ in appearance from her mate, but is rather smaller, and the white portions of her plumage are more or less tinged with grey; she can pipe, and will learn to talk and whistle almost as well as the male.

THE HUNTING CROW, *Cissa venatoria*, is one of the most beautiful members of this group of birds, as well as one of the most interesting: it is a native of India, and is occasionally imported in considerable numbers, but appears to be rather delicate, and does not usually survive its captivity for any length of time.

In size, the Hunting Crow about equals our English Magpie, but has a shorter tail; its strong beak and

legs are a bright orange-red; from either side of the
mouth a black band, embracing the eye, projects
backwards to the middle of the head, which is ornamented with a crest of long, narrow feathers, which
the bird has the power of raising up, but which it
usually carries lying flat. The whole plumage is of
a soft, silky texture—its general colour is sky-blue in
some specimens and sea-green in others; the wings
are chestnut colour with white spots, and the tail is
similarly marked. It is a gorgeous-looking creature,
and a great ornament to an aviary.

It is chiefly found in Nepaul and the Himalayas,
where it is sufficiently abundant and very frequently
domesticated. In confinement it may be fed as a
Jackdaw, giving more animal food, especially small
birds, which it plucks, feather by feather, before eating.
A large cage is necessary on account of the delicacy
of its feathers, and it should never be put in a dark
place, as light is indispensable for the preservation
of its beautiful colours, which quickly fade away and
become dull and dingy amid gloomy surroundings.

THE WANDERING PIE, *Dendrocitta vagabunda*, is
another member of this family that is well deserving
of the attention of amateurs, but space will not admit
of a detailed description. The same remarks will also
apply to the CHINESE BLUE PIE, *Urocissa sinensis;*
THE CHINESE BLUE MAGPIE, *Cyanopolius cyanus;*
THE SPANISH BLUE MAGPIE, *Cyanopolius cooki;* THE
BLUE-BEARDED JAY, *Cyanocorax cyanopogon*, and THE
PILEATED JAY, *Cyanocorax pileatus*, all of which are
handsome and lively birds, and not difficult to preserve
in confinement.

CHAPTER IV.

THE DOVE FAMILY
(Columbidæ).

The Cape Dove—The Barred Dove—The Graceful Ground Dove — The Barred-shouldered Dove — The Australian Crested Dove—The Blood-breasted Pigeon—The Indian Green-winged Pigeon—The Australian Green-winged Pigeon—The Bronze-spotted Dove—The Tambourine Pigeon—The Java Dove—The Egyptian Turtle Dove, &c.

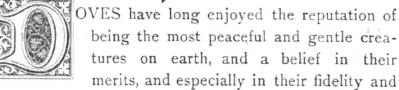OVES have long enjoyed the reputation of being the most peaceful and gentle creatures on earth, and a belief in their merits, and especially in their fidelity and affection for their mates and young, has long been current among mankind—so long, indeed, that I feel a natural repugnance to "hold the mirror up to nature" in their case and display them in their true colours, divested of the fictitious adornments wherewith they have been invested by inaccurate observers, at a time when little was known of natural history, and the imaginative descriptions of a few writers were accepted without questioning as

accurate, and handed down by successive generations of writers, who lacked either the leisure or the opportunity to investigate this subject for themselves, as veritable sun-pictures of which the fidelity was indisputable.

THE CAPE DOVE, *Œna capensis*, also very frequently called the Harlequin Dove, on account of the black mask, or "domino," worn by the adult male, is a pretty little bird, about the size of a skylark, but of slimmer build, and with a much longer tail.

As the English name implies, it comes to us from South Africa, and is one of the most desirable inmates of the columbarium. Care, however, must be taken not to lodge it with any of the larger or more pugnacious members of its family, by whom it would be speedily killed, for it is one of the most defenceless little creatures I have ever come across, permitting itself to be bullied to any extent by birds no bigger than a sparrow, without offering any resistance, or even remonstrance, beyond a little grunt and a slight raising of the wing.

The general colour is grey of several shades, and the male may be at once known by his black face. These birds nest freely in confinement, but the young are not always reared, for unless the weather is very warm, they die as soon as the old birds cease to brood them at night. They have not bred in my aviary, where they were too much disturbed by other birds, but have done so freely in that of a lady in the South of England, who thinks them the most delightful of Doves, "perfectly charming, but for the constantly recurring tragedy of their young." It is, however, satisfactory to find that patience had its appropriate reward, and that a pair of young Cape Doves were at length successfully reared to maturity, to rejoice their owner's heart by their gentleness and docility.

THE BARRED DOVE, *Geopelia striata* (see Fig. 3), is also known, especially in the trade, as the Zebra Dove. It is a native of India, and is a very pretty

FIG. 3.   THE BARRED DOVE.

bird, about the size of a thrush, and has bred at the "Zoo," as well as in several private aviaries. The plumage is, generally, fawn-grey, prettily marked with narrow, wavy black markings, from which its names are derived.

THE GRACEFUL GROUND DOVE, *Geopelia cuneata* (illustrated at Fig. 4), is also called the Diamond Dove. It is about the same size as the Barred Dove, but is of a light grey, prettily marked on the sides and

C

wings with black and white spots, whence its common English name. It is a native of Australia, but has reared young in the London Zoological Gardens.

FIG. 4. THE GRACEFUL GROUND DOVE.

THE BARRED-SHOULDERED DOVE, *Geopelia hume-ralis*, like the preceding species, is a native of Aus-tralia, and has also reproduced its kind at the "Zoo." It is a trifle larger than the two last-named species, but is equally attractive and desirable as an inmate of the aviary.

These small Doves are best fed on white millet, which is a kind of sorghum, dari, and canary-seed; hemp is objectionable, and care should be taken to supply them with an abundance of coarse grit, as well as a lump of rock-salt, and an unfailing supply of fresh water. Heather sprays form the best material for their nests, which are but slight affairs, and usually constructed on an artificial basis, such as the top of one of those small wicker cages in which so many canaries are brought over from Germany to this country.

THE AUSTRALIAN CRESTED DOVE, *Ocyphaps lophotes*, is a very delightful species, about the size of the common Barbary or Collared Turtle. As its name implies, its head is ornamented with an upstanding crest, constructed on the same principle as that of the cockatiel. The general colour is grey, with bronze reflections on the wings and neck, and the long, broad tail is prettily barred with white. When the bird alights on its perch it has a habit of slightly spreading and jerking up the tail, that is very curious. It is a ground-loving bird, and only resorts to the trees for sleeping purposes at night. In confinement, however, the Crested Dove's habits vary a good deal, and it passes much of its time dozing side by side with its mate on a branch.

The female bears a close resemblance to the male, but is decidedly smaller, and has a finer head and thinner neck. These birds breed freely in confinement, and I have known of one pair from which seventeen young were obtained in one season by giving their eggs to Collared Turtles to be hatched.

THE BLOOD-BREASTED PIGEON, *Phlogœnas cruentata*, is another fine species. It is a native of the Philippine Islands, and succeeds very well in confinement. Its English name is derived from a curious red spot on the centre of its white breast, which gives one the impression that the bird has just been stabbed, and that the mark in question is a stain of blood. It is a short, thick bird, about the size of a small Tumbler Pigeon.

C 2

THE INDIAN GREEN-WINGED PIGEON, *Chalcophaps indica* (illustrated at Fig. 5), is a very desirable bird, rather smaller than the last-named, but equally plump and compact in form. As its name implies, it is a native of our Indian Empire, where it is sufficiently common, but so hardy that it will pass the winter out-of-doors in this country without inconvenience. The breast is a delicate rosy or vinaceous tint, and the back and wings shine with metallic reflections.

FIG. 5.   THE INDIAN GREEN-WINGED PIGEON.

The female is smaller than her mate, and much duller in appearance. These pigeons have bred in confinement. Feed on any kind of small corn.

THE AUSTRALIAN GREEN-WINGED PIGEON, *Chalcophaps chrysochlora*, is readily distinguishable from the preceding species by its larger size and by a white mark above the bill; it is also quite hardy, and no doubt would breed in a suitable aviary, but it is not very frequently imported, and is consequently dear. It is a native of Northern Australia, and, like the preceding species, may be fed on any kind of small corn: those I had were especially fond of the round yellow maize.

THE BRONZE-SPOTTED DOVE, *Chalcopelia chalcospilos* (illustrated at Fig. 6), is a pretty, plump little thing, about the size of a quail. It is a native of Western Africa, and has occasionally bred in the

FIG. 6. THE BRONZE-SPOTTED DOVE.

aviary. Some that I had nested, but I found no eggs, and suspect the birds were all cocks, as the sexes are alike in outward appearance. Feed on white millet and canary-seed.

THE TAMBOURINE PIGEON, *Tympanistria bicolor* (illustrated at Fig. 7), is another little African Dove that derives its name from the peculiar note it utters, which is thought by some to resemble the sound made by tapping with the point of the finger on a tambourine,

but which is really more like that of water being
poured from a narrow-necked bottle. The male is
of a beautiful dark chocolate colour on the back and
wings, and snowy white on the neck, breast, and
belly. The female is generally like her mate, but is
smaller, and her white breast is flecked with grey.
Those I had nested in my aviary on the top of a

FIG. 7. THE TAMBOURINE PIGEON.

small cage, but did not lay. This and the preceding
species are decidedly tender, and must be taken
indoors during cold weather, which seems to paralyse
them, and soon throws them into a decline.

THE JAVA DOVE, *Turtur risorius,* var. *alba,* is
merely a white variety of the common Collared Dove,
which so many people will, erroneously, persist in

calling Ring-dove: it usually breeds true to colour, and will live outdoors all the year round.

THE EGYPTIAN TURTLE DOVE, *Turtur vinaceus*, is a fine, handsome bird, about half as large again as the preceding species, with which it will inter-breed and produce hybrids, which usually resemble the male bird, whose breast is ruddy fawn, back light chocolate, and top of head bluish. Feed on any kind of poultry mixture: it is quite hardy.

The following desirable species, of which space will not permit me to give a description, have all bred in the London Zoological Gardens, viz., THE WHITE-CROWNED PIGEON, *Columba leucocephala*, from the West Indies; THE PORTO RICO PIGEON, *C. corensis*, THE PICAZURO PIGEON, *C. picazuro*, and the BARE-EYED PIGEON, *C. gymnophthalma*—all West Indian species; and MAUGE'S DOVE, *Geopelia Maugæi*, which is a native of Australia.

The Turtles, including our common British species, *Turtur communis*, have all bred freely in the Gardens, and some of them in my own aviary. They are very handsome birds, but decidedly pugnacious, and require an aviary, or at least a compartment in the aviary, to themselves.

The genus *Peristera*, of which GEOFFROY'S DOVE is a well-known species, contains other hardy and beautiful birds, some of which are free breeders.

I can only name THE CROWNED and THE NICOBAR PIGEONS, the giants of their race, both in every way worthy of the attention of amateurs.

CHAPTER V.

THE DRONGO FAMILY
(*Dicruridæ*).

*The Drongo—Hottentot, Indian, or Great Rocket-
tailed Drongo.*

THE DRONGOES, of which there are several
varieties, form a family by themselves,
but are nearly related to the Crows,
Shrikes, and especially to the Flycatchers.
Linnæus classed them with the Shrikes, and Russ has
followed the great Swedish master in this respect,
naming the Drongo *Lanius hottentottus*, the specific
name probably having reference to the colour of the
bird, which is entirely of a dense shade of black, with
dark steel-blue reflections, which are chiefly apparent
in the full glare of the sun. The principal peculiarities of the Drongo, however, are found at the
opposite extremities of its body, the head being ornamented with a raised and somewhat incurved crest,
and the latter having two of its feathers much longer
than the rest, and terminated by a racket-shaped
expansion.

Some authorities place this bird among the Crows,

but its beak is scarcely corvine, nor are its legs and feet; so that they must have assigned the Drongo its position in the family *Corvidæ* solely on account of its raven-like plumage. The authorities at the "Zoo" have placed this bird between the Orioles and the Wood-swallows, to neither of which it bears much resemblance outwardly, though by the agile manner in which it captures its insect quarry on the wing, it rivals the latter in dexterity, equalling them in wing-power and quick sight.

THE HOTTENTOT DRONGO, *Chibia hottentotta*, is a very peculiar and most charming bird, constituting the genus *Chibia* of the family to which it belongs. It is a native of India, but why it should have received the specific name of *hottentotta* is one of those mysteries of avian nomenclature which are absolutely insoluble and incomprehensible.

The Hottentot Drongo certainly does not appear to think anything about its detestable name, but flies around, sings its melodious song, mimics all its neighbours, and passes its spare time catching flies, with the most supreme composure.

The song of this remarkable bird is not the least of its merits—it has some mellow and pleasing notes of its own—but it is the delightful and capable manner in which it imitates and appropriates to itself not only the songs of the other birds that are within hearing, but all kinds of domestic sounds, which it reproduces with no less fidelity to nature than added charm, that constitutes its merit as a songster—rivalling, if not indeed surpassing, the famous Mockingbird of the New World in this respect.

The female of this species is very nearly as good a performer as her decidedly talented husband, than whom she is a little more soberly clad. Drongoes are very quiet and inoffensive birds, and calmly allow themselves to be bullied by all kinds of feathered folk not half their size. They are about as large as a Fieldfare—only the long tail and the crest make the Drongoes look the larger of the two.

These birds are very seldom in the market, and when one does chance to be imported, the fortunate dealer demands a long price for his treasure. I recollect, some years ago, being asked £8 for one that had no tail and very few body feathers—a miserable-looking object indeed—and I declined to become its purchaser, not being at the time aware of its transcendent merits, which would really make it cheap at twice the money.

The following account of a Drongo from the pen of its fortunate owner, Mr. R. Phillipps, will no doubt be read with interest, as it enters into details which to me were inaccessible. Mr. Phillipps says: "I obtained 'Puck' two years ago, just after her arrival in this country. She had no tail then, and the flight feathers were worn away almost to the bone.

"I soon found that Puck, when in her house, would never go down for food. She came down too frequently—for she was perpetually trying to fly—and had no choice but to come down. No matter how hungry, however, she would hastily hop up to the highest perch; so I had to place her food on a shelf as high up as possible. When put on the floor

in the room, she would rush with frantic haste to
the lowest bar of the nearest chair ; and, while
crying piteously for mealworms, numbers crawling
a few inches below her would not entice her
down. She is a bird of the air, with an extraordinary
horror of the ground. Now that she is full-feathered
she is a different bird.

"When in the large garden aviary during the
summer, Puck is very keen after flies, taking them
cleverly on the wing. She is an excellent catch,
rarely losing a mealworm if there be plenty of flying
room, no matter how hard it may be thrown at her.
And food taken on the wing she swallows comfortably; whereas what is taken from a dish is
fumbled over, and often dropped. She is fond of
most dry insects, such as flies, mealworms, &c., and
small cockroaches in moderation. She cannot manage
raw, but is fond of cooked, meat. She is also fond
of dainties from the table—grapes and lettuce, often
eating a great deal of the latter. She drinks frequently, and washes in the drinking-water, but has
never been seen to take a regular bath.

"Puck is a capital mimic. Her favourite notes are a
selection from the song of the shâmah; but she is
equally conversant with the hoarse scream of the
offended jackdaw and the dulcet strains of the
neighbours' cats, with the gurgling bubbling of the
blue-cheeked barbet, and the plaintive whistle of the
blue robin. When whistling to herself she is specially
pretty, reminding one of the jolly plough-boy returning
home on a summer's evening. 'God Save the Queen'
she whistles sometimes quite correctly, but oftener

with variations according to the fancy of the moment. At one time she said 'Come along!' not unfrequently; and now often comes out with 'Pucky—Pucky!' When excited by the arrival of a strange bird, or by a visit from a lady with a striking bonnet, she gives utterance to various cries, jerking her tail up and down with great vehemence, at the same time opening and shutting the feathers like a large pair of shears.

"Puck is very sociable, and strongly objects to being left alone. She is never so happy as when being carried about on the finger, and petted. She comes to table for daylight meals, sitting straight and almost upright on the back of a chair. She is very observant, and peers about, passing remarks on everything that goes on. When she sees or hears me approaching, she receives me with fluttering wings, and sundry whistles and joyous calls Although over two years old, she behaves like a child, looking to us for everything, and crying for help when in distress.

"When sitting on her perch, Puck's extreme length seems to be 20in., of which the body is 7in., the tail proper 6in , the rackets extending 7in. beyond. A good crest curls back from the forehead over the crown. The feathers on the neck and shoulders form almost a mane; and when threatened by another bird, she holds her head very high, the beak down, and extends the mane sideways, uttering various uncanny sounds. The beak is large and arched, and the upper mandible, which overlaps the under-one, is plainly notched. The eight feathers of the ordinary tail form a fork. The two other and outer feathers hang separately, and are webbed to the same length as the others. The shafts are then more or less bare for some 4in., the remaining 3in. being webbed on one side of the shaft only. The colour of the bird is black, with a green gloss over the head, neck, throat, flights, and tail.

"Puck is an old maid, and is likely to remain one, for I have totally failed in my endeavours to obtain a mate for her. Perhaps this is well; for of favourite foreign birds she is quite the queen."

CHAPTER VI.

THE FINCH FAMILY
(*Fringillidæ*).

The Olive Finch—The Melodious Finch—The Diuca Finch—The Black Bullfinch—The St. Helena Seed-eater — The Grey Singing Finch — The Alario Finch — The Ruddy Finch — The Blood-stained Finch — The Totta Finch — Hartlaub's Finch — The White-throated Seed-eater.

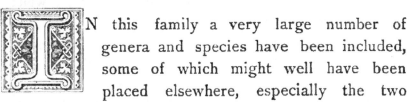I N this family a very large number of genera and species have been included, some of which might well have been placed elsewhere, especially the two species with which it is commenced in the "List" of the London Zoological Society—namely, the Indigo Bird and the Nonpareil.

In reviewing our British birds I restricted the use of the term "Finch" to those species which feed their young by regurgitating food from their crops, and I propose to follow the same course in this work, which will at once eliminate the above-mentioned birds, and a variety of others, some of which will be placed among the Sparrows, and others with he Mannikins and the Waxbills. One group has already been disposed of by itself—namely, the Cardinal family, which are included among the Finches by many writers, but are certainly quite distinct.

THE OLIVE FINCH, *Phonipara olivacea*, and THE MELODIOUS FINCH, *Phonipara canora*, may be bracketed together, as they differ mainly in size : the former inhabits Jamaica and the latter the larger island of Cuba. The Olive Finch is the bigger of the two birds, but the Melodious Finch has a sweeter note, and is also more amiable in a mixed aviary. It is about the size of a redpoll, the Olive Finch being a little larger. The colour in both is olivaceous-green and yellow, but the Melodious Finch has a brighter-tinted forehead. Both species make an open nest in a bush, and lay from three to five eggs of a bluish-white colour, speckled with blackish-brown. Their food in confinement should consist of millet (spray), white sorghum, and canary-seed.

THE DIUCA FINCH, *Diuca grisea*, is an unpretending-looking little grey bird, about the size of a linnet, darker above and lighter on the under-surface of the body. It is a native of Chili, and breeds freely in confinement, both in cage and aviary. It has a pretty little song, and is quite hardy. Treatment the same as that of the two preceding species.

THE BLACK BULLFINCH, *Melopyrrha nigra*, is stated in the Zoological Society's List to come from Cuba; but it is also a native of Brazil, whence the specimen in my possession was brought over by the gentleman who presented it to me. It is the size of a Bullfinch, with a large thick bill of a leaden-blue colour. The whole plumage, with the exception of a white bar on the wings, is jet-black. The female is smaller, and of a rusty-black or brownish colour. I am not aware if it has bred in confinement. The song is very sweet and melodious, but I can scarcely endorse my friend's opinion that "the 'Bicudo' is the best songster in the world." It was supposed to be delicate, and required to be kept very warm: under these conditions my bird became entirely bare, but regained its plumage when placed in a cooler situation than the kitchen, where I had been advised to put it.

THE ST. HELENA SEED-EATER, or GREEN SINGING FINCH, *Crithagra butyracea,* is a South African species, acclimatised at St. Helena, whence most of those seen in this country are imported. It is a very pretty little bird, about the size of a Siskin. The breast is yellow, the back greyish, and the eye surmounted by a narrow streak of bright yellow. The female only differs from her mate by being a trifle smaller and generally duller in colour. This species has bred mules with the canary, and rears its own young very freely in confinement, making an open nest in a bush or in a nest-box. It is a delightful songster. Food: canary-seed, millet, and sorghum.

THE GREY SINGING FINCH, *Crithagra musica,* is a pretty little creature—grey above, with white under-parts. It is a native of Western Africa, and is, if possible, a sweeter singer than the preceding species, and should be fed and treated like it. This bird has bred in confinement, but I am not aware of any mules having been obtained from it, though such should not be impossible.

THE ALARIO FINCH, *Fringilla alario*, classed among the Sparrows in the Zoological List, has bred mules with the canary, as well as reproduced its own species in captivity. It is not a handsome bird, being disfigured by a black face (whence the German name of Masked Finch); the rest of the body is brown and white—the latter colour on the lower, and the former on the upper parts of the body. The female is greyish-brown above, and whitish-grey on the under-surface.

THE RUDDY FINCH, *Carpodacus erythrinus,* is a native of Siberia, and is a very desirable addition to the aviary. It will pair and breed freely with its own species or with other members of the Finch family.

THE BLOOD-STAINED FINCH, *Carpodacus hæmorrhous,* which is also called the Purple Finch, *Fringilla purpurea* (Audubon), is a native of Mexico, and a very good aviary bird. It has produced mules with a canary in the aviary of a gentleman at Lewes, who is an adept in the art of obtaining hybrids of all kinds.

THE TOTTA FINCH, *Loxia* or *Fringilla totta,* is another nice little bird, bearing a general family likeness to the foregoing, but distinguishable by its blackish-brown tail. One was exhibited some time ago, and took a prize at a leading show, as a Bullfinch Siskin mule! Needless to say, it is a perfectly distinct species, and not a cross of any sort, and is common about the Cape. In size it is rather larger than a Siskin, and is susceptible of being made very tame, but is less noticeable for its musical accomplishments than some of its congeners.

D

All these birds should be fed alike on sorghum, canary, and millet-seed; they also require a plentiful supply of sharp grit.

Other desirable members of the Finch family remain, but space will not permit me to mention more than the two foremost of them, viz., HARTLAUB'S FINCH, *F. Hartlaubi* (Russ), otherwise *Crithagra chrysopyga*, and THE WHITE-THROATED SEED-EATER, *C. albogularis*, both from South-western Africa, and requiring the same treatment as those already described.

CHAPTER VII.

THE KINGFISHER FAMILY
(*Alcedinidæ*).

The Laughing Jackass—The Australian Kingfisher—
The Ternate Kingfisher.

HIS family, of which our well-known English Kingfisher is a typical representative, contains some choice species very suitable for the aviary.

THE LAUGHING JACKASS, *Dacelo gigantea*, is a remarkably fine bird, well known to Australian colonists. Its cry or call is very curious, and resembles something between the braying of a donkey and a very loud laugh.

While bearing a general likeness to the head of the family, the Laughing Jackass nevertheless differs materially, especially as regards size and brilliancy of colouring, from our English Kingfisher; but all the same it is a handsome creature, and the crest on its head, which it has the power of raising or depressing at will, gives it quite a distinguished appearance.

In size it is a large bird, measuring about 18in. in length, but the legs are short, and it progresses only indifferently well upon the ground. With regard to its dietary in its native woods, the Laughing Jackass may be considered a most useful creature to mankind, for it subsists on snakes, lizards, and noxious insects, such as centipedes, scorpions, large caterpillars, and so forth, of which it consumes an enormous quantity, for the intestinal canal being short, digestion proceeds with great rapidity, so that an hour or so after it has swallowed say a snake as long as itself, the Laughing Jackass is quite ready for another meal.

The crest is black, shaded with brown, and the rest of the upper surface is brownish-olive; the wings, however, are brownish-black, some of the wing coverts presenting reflections of green and blue; the breast and belly are white, with bars of pale brown across the former. The long tail is chestnut-brown, with a band of black towards the lower third of the feathers, which are tipped with white.

In the house it may be fed on meat (raw preferably), frogs when procurable, insects of all kinds, snails and slugs, and small dead birds: the last-named it will greedily devour, though in its wild state it does not prey on birds or animals, but solely on reptiles and insects. Being a large bird, and eating and voiding copiously, the Dacelo is not well adapted to cage-life; but in a large aviary it will do very well, and after the first cold season in this country—when it should be taken into the house—it may be safely wintered out of doors. I have heard of no instance in which it has bred in confinement

THE AUSTRALIAN KINGFISHER, *Halcyon sancta*, which replaces the preceding species in Northern

Australia, is about the same size, but far more brilliantly coloured: the head and scapularies are green, the throat, neck, and abdomen buff, abundantly flecked with brown spots. The wings and tail are greenish-blue, and the ear-coverts and a line round the back of the head are very dark green. Treatment the same as for the preceding species.

THE TERNATE KINGFISHER, *Tanysiptera dea*, is a magnificent bird from New Guinea, as yet of very infrequent occurrence here, but one that will doubtless be imported freely by-and-bye, when its native land has been more fully opened up to commerce. It is chiefly distinguishable for the great length of the central pair of tail feathers, which have each a racket-like expansion at the extremity.

All the Kingfishers that, like the foregoing, live in dry forests far from water, are susceptible of being kept in confinement without much difficulty.

CHAPTER VIII.

THE LARK FAMILY
(*Alaudidæ*).

The Chinese Lark—The Black Lark—The Short-toed Lark—The Madras Bush-Lark—The Thick-billed Lark—The Bullfinch-headed Lark.

HIS is not a numerous family anywhere, and its foreign members are much less meritorious subjects for introduction to the aviary than our own species, still THE CHINESE LARK, *Melanocorypha mongolica*, from Central Asia, is a nice bird, as also are THE BLACK LARK, *M. yeltoniensis*, from Siberia, THE SHORT-TOED LARK, *Calandrella brachydactyla*, from Northern Africa, and THE MADRAS BUSH-LARK, *Mirafra affinis*, from India; but they are all of such very rare occurrence in the bird-shops that the bare mention of their names here will be sufficient. If obtained, however, they may be fed on the food provided for our English Larks.

THE THICK-BILLED LARK and THE BULLFINCH-HEADED LARK have both been seen at shows, but are of even rarer occurrence than the above.

CHAPTER IX.

THE MANNIKIN FAMILY
(*Muniidæ*).

The Bengali—The Nutmeg Bird—The White-headed Nun—The Black-headed Nun—The Three-coloured Nun—The Silverbill—The Bronze-winged Mannikin—The Bar-breasted Mannikin—The Chestnut-bellied Mannikin—The Topela Mannikin.

ANNIKINS form a numerous group, of which the limits of the present work will only permit of my passing in review the principal species, and I propose commencing with the sub-group of Mannikins proper, which are distinguished by the curious habit of singing in dumb show; that is to say, the bird will go through all the motions of a songster in full swing, and yet to the ordinary spectator not a sound will be audible.

THE BENGALI, or BENGALESE, *Munia acuticauda*, occurs in three principal varieties—namely, the white, the white and fawn, and the white and brown. These little birds, especially the first of them (which is illustrated at Fig. 8), are essentially birds for the cage, in which they breed as freely as canaries, and with much less fuss as to elaboration of food, seeing that their diet consists mainly of white sorghum, commonly called millet, upon which they also feed their young.

Fig. 8. The White Bengalese.

They all make a nest of hay, lined with cotton and feathers, in a cocoanut husk, or shell, a small cage,

Fig. 9. The Nutmeg Bird.

or any convenient box. They lay four or five pure white eggs, which are incubated for twelve or thirteen days, and there are numerous broods during the year.

Occasionally they fail to bring up the young; but as a rule, if not interfered with, they make good parents. It is not well to turn them suddenly adrift into a large aviary, as their powers of flight are but limited, and being of a timid disposition, they would be in danger of being bullied by their stronger and bolder companions. They are rather smaller than a redpoll, and are usually imported from China.

THE NUTMEG BIRD, *Munia punctularia* (illustrated

FIG. 10.   THE WHITE-HEADED NUN.

at Fig. 9), an Indian species, but of frequent occurrence in dealers' shops, is about the same size as the last, and is a very pretty bird. The head and back are rich brown, the under-surface being marked with numerous white spots on a light-coloured brown ground. Male and female are alike, and are quite hardy, living in confinement for some ten years. They have never bred in this country.

THE WHITE-HEADED NUN, or MAJA FINCH, *Munia maja* (illustrated at Fig. 10), is an exceedingly pretty bird of a soft chestnut-brown all over except the head and upper part of the neck, which are creamy white, and the under-tail coverts, which are black. Male and female are alike. It has not bred in England.

THE BLACK-HEADED NUN, *Munia malacca,* is the counterpart of the last species, except that its head is black; it also wants the dark under-tail coverts.

THE THREE-COLOURED NUN, *Munia sinensis,* is another bird belonging to this group. It has a leaden-grey bill; black head, neck, and shoulders; white breast and sides; brown back, wings, and tail; and black vent and under-tail coverts; legs and feet lead colour.

FIG. 11. THE SILVERBILL.

All the foregoing are quiet, amiable little creatures that delight to live in company, and will sit in rows side by side without moving for an hour at a time, each singing in dumb show, one after the other, while all the rest listen most attentively to what is, no doubt, an audible melody to them.

THE SILVERBILL, *Munia cantans* (illustrated at Fig. 11), is a small bird, about the size of a wren, but with a larger tail and more slender form. It differs from the other members of the family by the possession of an audible and exceedingly sweet song, and, unlike the Nuns, it breeds freely in the aviary, but is just as amiable as they are. The upper part is fawn colour, the wings and tail are a shade darker, and the lower part of the body is greyish-white; the bill is bluish-grey with a silvery tinge, whence the name. Food: millet, sorghum, and canary-seed.

THE BRONZE-WINGED MANNIKIN, or HOODED FINCH, *Munia cucullata* (illustrated at Fig. 12), is a pretty little bird, smaller than any of the preceding

FIG. 12. THE BRONZE-WINGED MANNIKIN.

The head is black, as are also the throat, wings, and back, but shining with various shades of metallic sheen; the chest is white. Male and female are alike, and will breed freely in the aviary. Feed like the preceding.

There are several other less known species, which space will only permit me to name, viz., THE BAR-BREASTED MANNIKIN, *M. nisoria;* THE CHESTNUT-BELLIED MANNIKIN, *M. rubro-nigra;* THE TOPELA MANNIKIN, or FINCH, *M. topela,* &c.

CHAPTER X.

THE OWL FAMILY
(*Asionidæ*).

The Scops Owl—The Passerine Owl—The Prairie, Burrowing, or Coquimbo Owl.

S a rule, these "midnight prowlers," these "feathered cats," are not looked upon in the light of domestic pets; but as they are not quite ignored by the venerable Bechstein in his ever-admirable "History of Chamber Birds," I have decided to give them a short chapter to themselves in the present work, for they are great favourites with some people, and, when rightly understood and properly treated, make really quite charming pets. The larger species, such as THE EAGLE OWL, *Bubo maximus*, and its allies, THE LONG-EARED OWL, *Asio otus*, THE SHORT-EARED OWL, *A. brachyotis*, and their congeners, are outside the scope of this volume; but THE SCOPS OWL, *Scops giu*, THE PASSERINE OWL, *Glaucidium passerinum*, and THE PRAIRIE OWL, otherwise called the BURROWING OWL, *Speotyto cunicularia*, merit at least a passing notice; for the two first, though

European species, do not often occur in these Islands—
of their own free will, at all events—and the third is a
South American species that from the date of its
first discovery by Europeans has attracted the attention of naturalists in no small degree from its peculiar habits.

THE SCOPS OWL, *Scops giu,* is found in considerable numbers in the South of Europe, on the
borders of the Mediterranean, and is very docile and
amusing in confinement, for it comes forth at twilight
and flies about lightly and swiftly, catching moths and
other nocturnal insects on the wing. It is a charming
little bird, about the size of a missel thrush, and nests
freely in confinement, though the young are not
always reared. Its diet consists of meat, especially
the flesh of small birds; insects, such as moths,
mealworms, and cockroaches; and ants' eggs, upon
which it will thrive and live for a long time in health
and contentment.

Mr. R. Phillipps, a close observer as well as a
great lover of birds, sends me the following interesting account for publication. He says:—" One is
apt to associate the Owl with a ferocious, bloodthirsty
creature, but the Scops is a very gentle little fellow,
and need not alarm the most timid of bird-lovers.
When young, Scops Owls fly so gently, so butterfly-
like, that it seems as if they never could be strong
of flight; but the adult birds are strong and rapid
on the wing—as, indeed, they have need to be, for
they feed largely on moths, which they catch cleverly
in the air.

" The Scops is an insect-eater, and will pounce on

a mealworm, beetle, grasshopper, or cockroach, with all the grandeur, in its little way, of an eagle on a hare. It rarely eats its prey on the ground, but carries it to a neighbouring perch. Although settling on the ground without hesitation, it never—at any rate, if in good condition and in a large aviary—hops or walks, and should it swallow a small insect on the ground and wish to seize another only a few inches distant, it will invariably rise a little in the air and make a second pounce.

"Perhaps when young these birds are more comical than at any other period of their existence. On the approach of a stranger, or of anything they may consider to be dangerous, they lengthen themselves out, raise their horns, and become perfectly rigid, hiding themselves (and successfully, too) behind any upright stick or branch. The bird then looks more like some stuffed enormity than a living creature.

"I have had the young and the adult birds, and find them exceedingly easy to tame, not only feeding from the hand, but flying towards me on my appearance, and sitting quietly on the finger.

"My Scops-eared Owls lay freely every summer in some box or barrel, and sit steadily; but the eggs have always been clear. For a long time they have been kept in the same aviary with various large and not over-amiable birds. Of a pair of White Jackdaws they are specially afraid, and retire to rest so very early in the morning, and rise so very late in the evening, to avoid these spiteful companions, that their feeding-hours have been reduced to a minimum, and may well account for unfertile eggs. The younger birds seem to lay three or four eggs, and the fully-developed birds six, in June. The eggs are white, round, a little coarse in the grain, and very large for the size of the bird.

"I feed my Scops on raw meat or sheep's heart cut small, sometimes with a little cooked meat added. This I place in a small flower-pot saucer on a shelf where it may be easily found. Mealworms and cockroaches are given from time to time. They also feed occasionally from the other birds' saucers. They cannot tear up large pieces of meat sufficiently to sustain life, and are often slow, especially when young and in a large aviary, to find their feeding-saucers. These two points must be borne in mind, or your Scops will fill their stomachs with rubbish and die of atrophy. I leave these birds out summer and winter, except in very severe weather, when I take them in as a precautionary measure; but then they have plenty of room to fly about in, and shelters from rain and every wind. They drink regularly, and wash in the ordinary washing-pans.

"The Scops-eared Owl is very pleasingly marked with various shades of brown and reddish-brown, but varies according to the age: some specimens are much redder than others, and some grey. My birds, measured while sitting on a perch, seem to be nearly 7in. long; the breadth is considerable. When young, and afterwards in a less degree, the lower part of the iris is orange, the upper yellow. The horns are conspicuous only when the bird is alarmed. It is exceedingly difficult to distinguish the sexes; usually, but not always, the male is the smaller, wilder, and more deeply marked round the face, and has a slimmer appearance than his mate."

THE PASSERINE OWL, *Glaucidium passerinum*, is about the same size as the last species, and, like it, inhabits the southern parts of Europe, occurring at rare intervals in the British Islands, where, of course, it is invariably caught or destroyed as soon as seen. In confinement it should be fed on small mice and birds cut into pieces with the hair or feathers left on, as the hair of the mice and the feathers of the birds have a beneficial effect on the Owls, which seem to need a cleansing process in their interior. They do not thrive on a dietary of which they are unable to reject a portion in the form of pellets; but when they are "sick" after eating, they are in good health. I have not heard of their having bred in this country, either in the woods or in captivity.

The eggs are two or three in number, of a white colour, and the male and female take turn about to incubate them; the nest is usually placed in a hollow tree The young are said to be readily brought up by hand, if care is taken to feed them at night and not during the day, when they are sleepy and sometimes will not open their mouths.

THE PRAIRIE, BURROWING, or COQUIMBO OWL, *Speotyto cunicularia*, or *Athene cunicularia* (Wood), is a native of the New World, and is well known by reputation to bird-fanciers, if not as frequently imported as many less interesting species. It makes a very nice pet, and is capable of being perfectly tamed. It is nearly twice as large as either of the two species just described, and should be fed and treated in the same manner. It is, however, somewhat impatient of cold, and should be carefully guarded against sudden changes of temperature; while some attempt should be made to reproduce for its benefit in captivity the conditions under which it exists "at home," where contrary to all analogy, and even to what might naturally be deduced from its appearance, it makes its dwelling under ground, sometimes in burrows of its own construction, but more frequently in those of the prairie-dog, a species of marmot very abundant on the plains of South America.

The Prairie Owl is not, perhaps, as strictly nocturnal in its habits as most of its congeners, but nevertheless gets confused and frightened if suddenly exposed to a strong light, when the pupils of its eyes contract to mere slits of a hair's breadth, like those of the domestic cat under similar circumstances.

The remarkably long legs of this Owl are thickly covered with minute, hair-like feathers down to the insertion of the talons; although in its native haunts it is not exposed to inclement weather, such as the Owls of the northern hemisphere have to encounter : the reason for the covering, therefore, is not apparent.

The colouring of the Prairie Owl is rather pleasing, consisting as it does of several shades of brown— prettily disposed, and darker on the upper than on the lower parts of the body—which have a greyish tinge. One that I kept for some time was very fond of mice, but would eat meat, and preferred it raw. It would not touch insects, such as blackbeetles and mealworms, though some naturalists assert the species to be at least partially insectivorous. Small birds were

E

greedily devoured, and were invariably plucked before being consumed. Mice, if small, were swallowed whole, but those of a larger size were dismembered, and no part was left, the fur and bones being afterwards cast up in little pellets, after the manner of all predaceous birds. It both drank and bathed, and was always more lively in the dusk of the morning and evening than at other times, retiring in the day to the darkest corner of its den, where it was accustomed to sit on a half-brick in preference to a wooden perch, with which it was also provided.

CHAPTER XI.

THE PARROT FAMILY
(*Psittacidæ*).

The Budgerigar — The Red-faced Love-Bird — The Peach-faced Love-Bird—The Grey-headed Love-Bird—The Cockatiel—The Turquoisine—The Grey Parrot—Amazon Parrots—Cockatoos—Macaws—Indian Parrakeets—The Hawk-headed Parrot—Conures—The Quaker Parrakeet, &c.

AT the "Zoo" this "family" constitutes an "order," *Psittaci*, which is divided into four sub-families, to the last only of which is allotted the designation I prefer for the whole group and have affixed to the head of this chapter. The other three are THE COCKATOOS, *Cacatuidæ*, which is made to include THE COCKATIEL; THE NIGHT PARROTS, *Stringopidæ;* and THE LONG-TAILED PARROTS, *Palæornithidæ;* while in the fourth sub-family, "*Psittacidæ*," are included THE LOVE-BIRDS, THE BROADTAILS, THE AMAZONS, THE CONURES, and a host of other genera and species.

THE BUDGERIGAR, *Melopsittacus undulatus*, which is also known by the name of Shell Parrot, Undulated

Grass Parrakeet, and Warbling Grass Parrakeet, is
a native of South Australia, and breeds as freely
in confinement as a canary—a well-grown specimen
of which familiar bird it about equals in size, though
its longer tail and shorter legs give it a quite different
appearance, as will be seen on reference to Fig. 13.
The general colour is vivid grass-green, the forehead

FIG. 13. THE BUDGERIGAR.

is primrose, and the back and wings are marked with
a number of blackish undulating lines that have caused
some naturalists to give it the name of Zebra Parrakeet; the cere, or naked skin about the nostrils, is
sky-blue in the male and cream coloured in the female,
unless when she is nesting, when it turns brown. The
proper food is millet and canary-seed, to which oats

and soaked bread may be added when there are any young ones to be fed.

The eggs are white, and vary from three to nine in number; they are incubated in about sixteen days, and the young hatch out in succession, so that as much as eight days may intervene between the birth of the oldest and the youngest member of the little family. A cocoanut husk makes a capital nesting-place: it should be hung up out of reach of mice,

FIG. 14. THE RED-FACED LOVE-BIRD.

and have the aperture, which should be at one end, turned towards the light.

The usual time for these birds to moult is in June or July; when the moult is over—generally in August—they commence to breed, and continue to rear brood after brood until about Christmas. They are perfectly hardy, and may be kept all the year round in a properly-constructed aviary out of doors, in which they will do much better than if confined in a cage indoors. They will live for twelve or fifteen years in the house.

THE RED-FACED LOVE-BIRD, *Agapornis pullaria* (illustrated at Fig. 14), is a general favourite. It is very different in appearance from the preceding species, being short and squat of figure, with a short, broad tail. The general colour is green, the forehead and face orange-red, and the tail barred with red and black. It is a native of South-western Africa, is about the size of a bullfinch, and has not bred in confinement. It should be fed on boiled maize, and may also have canary-seed and millet; but if fed on the two last alone, it will soon fall into a decline and die.

THE PEACH-FACED LOVE-BIRD, *Agapornis roseicollis*, which bears a general likeness to the last-named species, is also a native of South-western Africa. It is, however, larger, being about the size of a Siberian bullfinch, and its face, instead of being red, is of a delicate peach-bloom colour. The tail is marked in a similar manner to that of the Red-face, but the beak, which in the latter is reddish-orange, has a greenish-white tinge in the former. The Red-face is a very silent bird, but the Peach-face is an exceedingly noisy little creature; and when it chatters, its tail bobs up and down keeping time with its rapidly-repeated note.

This species breeds freely in confinement, but the sexes are so exactly alike in appearance that it is difficult to get a pair. The best nest is a small hollow log with a hole at one end; it should be fixed sidewise in such a manner that mice cannot reach it. Feed as recommended for the Red-face. Both these birds are fairly hardy, but cannot be kept out of doors all the year round.

THE GREY-HEADED LOVE-BIRD, *Agapornis cana*, is a native of Madagascar, and is a very nice little thing ; it is about the same size as the Red-faced Love-Bird. The head and neck of the male is of a delicate pearl-grey colour; the rest of the body is green, except the tail, which is barred with black. The female is

FIG. 15. THE COCKATIEL.

all green. Feed and treat like the two preceding species. It is hardy, and may be kept out of doors all the year round ; sometimes it breeds in confinement.

THE COCKATIEL, *Calopsitta novæ hollandiæ*, of which an illustration is given at Fig. 15, is a very charming bird, about twice as large as the preceding species. Its tail is long, and its head is ornamented with a crest. The general colour is ash-grey, with a bar of white across each wing. The face of the male is yellow, which distinguishes him from the female; the tail of the latter is also marked profusely with narrow yellow bars on the under-surface, while that of the male is black. Both sexes have a small patch of a brick-red colour on the side of the face.

FIG. 16. THE TURQUOISINE.

This species breeds very freely in confinement. Both birds sit on the eggs—the male during the day, the female at night. Incubation lasts about seventeen days, and the number of young varies from three to seven. There are about four broods during the season, which extends from May to October, the female frequently beginning to lay again before the little ones have left the nest. These birds are perfectly hardy. Feed as recommended for the Love-Birds, adding oats and bread.

THE TURQUOISINE, *Euphema pulchella* (illustrated at Fig. 16), from New South Wales, is intermediate in size between the Budgerigar and the Cockatiel; it breeds as freely in confinement as either of them, and requires the same treatment. Its general colour is dark green, with turquoise-blue markings on the face,

FIG. 17. THE ROSELLA PARRAKEET.

a yellowish shade on the lower parts of the body, and a patch of dull red on the shoulder. The sexes do not differ much in appearance, but the female shows less of the blue and red than her mate.

Among the Broadtails, *Platycerci*, I may mention THE REDRUMP, THE ROSELLA (illustrated at Fig. 17), THE PILEATED PARRAKEET, THE PENNANT and

BAUER'S and BARNARD'S PARRAKEETS, as very desirable birds, regretting that I can do no more than name any of them.

There are some very interesting Parrots in New Zealand, among which I may mention THE GOLDEN-CROWNED and the RED-FRONTED PARRAKEETS. The latter is quite hardy, and will breed, often quite freely, in confinement.

THE GREY PARROT, *Psittacus erithacus* (illustrated at Fig. 18), makes a most charming pet. Docile and affectionate to a degree when rationally treated, it is the best talker of any bird known, and lives to a good age, even passing from generation to generation of human owners as a living heirloom.

For the benefit of the few who are unacquainted with the bird, I may say that the head, neck, breast, and back are of a light ashen-grey colour; the wings a darker grey; the middle and lower part of the back and the rump are greyish-white; the tail, as well as upper- and lower-tail coverts, scarlet; breast, belly, sides, and hinder part of the body, whitish-grey; the beak, black; the eyes, black, grey, yellow, or white, according to age; the skin on the nose and a circle round the eye (eye cere), featherless and greyish-white; the feet, bluish or whitish-grey, dappled with black; the claws, black. The plumage of both male and female is the same, and, like that of most Parrots, more or less full of down. These birds vary much in size, but the average length from tip of beak to end of tail is from 14in. to 15½in.

Newly-imported Grey Parrots are subject to extraordinary mortality, owing to the unhealthy way in which they are usually brought over. In the first place, they mostly perform the journey from their native land to this country in the dark and intensely hot hold of a steamship, where they are greatly overcrowded. Their food is thrown on the floor of the box in which they are confined, and they have to

FIG. 18. THE GREY PARROT.

pick it up and eat it contaminated with their own droppings, which, amidst the intense heat, soon become putrid, and implant the germs of sure and certain death in the poor prisoners. As a rule, they are given no water, so that their raging thirst compels them to swallow the semi-liquid abominations on the floor of their prison; and under these circumstances there is nothing to be wondered at in the small per-centage of Grey Parrots that live after their arrival in this country, for, in addition to typhoid fever and diphtheria, which are already at work in their systems owing to the treatment they have received, they con-tract bronchitis and inflammation of the lungs, and not one in a hundred newly-imported birds survives twelve months. It behoves the reader, therefore, in purchasing a Grey Parrot, to be very careful to see that he is obtaining one that is thoroughly healthy and acclimatised.

Few persons seem to know how to treat Grey Parrots. As a rule, the poor birds get fed on " scraps from the table," "bread soaked in tea, coffee, or milk," and not infrequently they are deluged with water "because they will not bathe"; whereas they roll in sand or dust like larks and chickens. They get no wood to nibble—a necessity for Parrots which are born whittlers—and no small stones to aid them in the digestion of their food. In addition, many fanciers deprive the poor things of water, and force them, for the sake of the moisture it contains, to eat "sop," until they die from indigestion, owing to over-distension of the crop.

For food, a Grey Parrot requires boiled maize (fresh every day, for it soon turns sour), hemp- and canary-seed (which some, however, will not touch at first), a crust of dry bread, and occasionally a little ripe fruit or a few nuts. "Sop" should be most carefully avoided, as the traditional diet of bread and milk is an abomination. No animal food should be given, inclusive of butter or grease of any kind, or even puddings containing egg or milk.

THE AMAZON PARROTS, a South American genus, form a large group in themselves, the principal species being THE BLUE-FRONTED, *Chrysotis æstiva*, which is distinguished by a circlet of blue on the forehead, immediately above the insertion of the upper mandible; THE FESTIVE AMAZON, *C. festiva*, which is known by a red patch above the tail, both of which,

FIG. 19. THE LEADBEATER COCKATOO.

and especially the latter, make very good talkers, though some fanciers award the palm in this respect to LEVAILLANT'S, or THE DOUBLE-FRONTED AMAZON, *C. levaillanti*, a bird readily known by its primrose-coloured head and neck, and THE GOLDEN-NAPED AMAZON, *C. auripalliata*, which has many admirers. Many other species are spoken of with approval by those who have kept them.

The best staple food for all the Amazon Parrots is hemp-seed, which may be varied with ripe fruit, plain biscuit, and nuts now and then. It is needless to remark that all Parrots should have water to drink, and a piece of soft wood on which to exercise their beaks, the want of which often impels them to pluck out their feathers and make themselves anything but a "joy for ever."

THE COCKATOOS are a numerous and noisy race, but

FIG. 20. THE ROSE-BREASTED COCKATOO.

general favourites nevertheless. A lady of my acquaintance once had as many as fifteen of them, among which were two GREAT SALMON-CRESTED MOLUCCAN COCKATOOS, *Cacatua moluccensis*, a BLUE-EYED COCKATOO, *C. ophthalmica*, and a BARE-EYED COCKATOO, *C. gymnopis*, the latter a wonderful talker. Among the others were a NOSEY COCKATOO, *Licmetis tenuirostris*, also an accomplished bird; a LEADBEATER

COCKATOO, *C. leadbeateri* (illustrated at Fig. 19), a magnificent creature with a tri-coloured crest, and a plumage reminding one of raspberries and cream; and a ROSE-BREASTED COCKATOO, *Cacatua roseicapilla*, (of which an illustration is given at Fig. 20). This was also a handsome bird, with a pinky-white

FIG. 21. THE GREAT WHITE COCKATOO.

short crest, grey back, wings, and tail, and a roseate breast and lower parts. In the case of this Cockatoo, however, it was not one of "handsome is that handsome does," for its yells were simply demoniacal.

My favourite Cockatoo is GOFFIN'S, *C. goffini*, from the Solomon Islands, but many people prefer THE

AUSTRALIAN LEMON-CREST, *C. galerita*, whilst some extol THE SULPHUR-CREST, *C. sulphurea*, a bantam among the Cockatoos, for it is no bigger than a Grey Parrot, and others THE GREAT WHITE COCKATOO, *C. cristata* (illustrated at Fig 21). This latter is the largest of the Cockatoo family, and is not a bad talker, but its cries are deafening.

THE MACAWS, *Arinæ*, I have not said anything about, and do not intend to enlarge upon their merits and demerits, for they are too big to be general favourites, and not sufficiently intelligent to compensate for their destructive habits and intolerable shrieks.

THE INDIAN PARRAKEETS, *Palæornithinæ*, are well known—perhaps the longest if not the best known of all their race; but I cannot say much in their praise. THE ALEXANDRINE is a fine big fellow, but no beauty, while THE RING-NECK, *Palæornis torquatus*, is pretty enough, but decidedly treacherous; THE BLOSSOM-HEAD, *P. cyanocephalus*, on the other hand, is docile and pretty, but stupid, as a rule; and the remaining members of the group, including the rare MALACCAN or LONG-TAILED PARRAKEET, *P. longicauda*, and HODGSON'S PARRAKEET, *P. Hodgsoni* (Russ), call for no special remark.

The Ring-neck and the Blossom-head have both bred in captivity.

Hemp, canary-seed, plain biscuit, maize, and nuts, with clean water, coarse grit, and soft wood, will keep them all in health and condition for many years.

THE HAWK-HEADED PARROT, *Deroptyus accipitrinus*, is, without exception, the most delightful member of the whole family; it is not a common species, even

in Brazil, its native place, but I have had the
good fortune to possess two examples, a female and
a male, and perfect gems they are, as tame as tame
can be, very hardy and healthy, wonderful mimics,
good whistlers, and very fair talkers.

The illustration (see Fig. 22) will give a good idea of
the peculiar feature of the plumage—the ruff round the

FIG. 22.   THE HAWK-HEADED PARROT

neck, which is erectile at will and of a purple-red hue
with blue tips to the feathers; the same arrangement
of colour prevails on the breast; the back, wings, and
tail are rich green; the head grey-white, and the face
dark grey; each feather is striped down the centre with
a yellowish-white stripe, and the whole arrangement
of the plumage gives the bird a decidedly hawk-like

F

appearance, but there the likeness ends, for it is one of the most gentle and playful of Parrots, and one that I can heartily recommend to fanciers in search of an intelligent, handsome, and most amusing pet.

THE CONURES, or WEDGE-TAILED PARROTS, classed at the "Zoo" with the Macaws, are a very distinct group, placed by some writers in a separate sub-family under the designation *Conurinæ*, which fits passing well. The most conspicuous are THE GOLDEN CONURE, *C. luteus*, which, as its name implies, is of a golden-yellow colour generally, but has a white bill and green wings; it is very rare and expensive, but a delightful bird. THE YELLOW CONURE, *C. solstitialis*, also called THE SUN PARRAKEET; THE NANDAY, *C. nanday*, a green bird with a black head; THE JENDAYA CONURE, *C. jendaya*, which rings the changes in red and yellow and green, and is much sought after by amateurs who love gaudy plumage; and THE WHITE-EARED CONURE, *C. leucotis*, which is an exceedingly pretty little bird, much smaller than any of the preceding; but I must warn amateurs against it, and indeed all the Conures, except the Golden, as they are very spiteful in a mixed aviary, and will remorselessly persecute and kill birds twice their size—as I found to my cost.

THE QUAKER PARRAKEET, *Bolborhynchus monachus*, has been separated from its allies and placed in a genus by itself, possibly on account of its nest-building proclivities. It is curious that it should have made such a wide departure from the habits of the race as to build itself a nest of sticks in a tree; but it has. As the Quaker Parrakeet is a very free breeder

in confinement and a gentle and tamable bird to boot,
it can be recommended to the notice of amateurs in
spite of its propensity for screaming, which, however,
is seldom indulged in when several Bolborhynchi are
kept together.

The genus *Pionus* contains some nice birds, notably
THE RED-VENTED PARROT, *P. menstruus;* THE
DUSKY PARROT, *P. violaceus;* THE WHITE-HEADED
PARROT, *P. senilis;* and MAXIMILIAN'S PARROT,
P. maximiliani.

In the genus *Brotogerys* we have THE ALL-GREEN
PARRAKEET, *Brotogerys tiriacula,* which is a very
charming creature; THE CANARY-WINGED PARRAKEET,
B. virescens; THE GOLDEN-FRONTED PARRAKEET,
B. tuipara; THE TOVI PARRAKEET, *B. tovi;* and
THE ORANGE-WINGED PARRAKEET, *B. xanthopterus,*
which are all natives of South America, fairly hardy
and inexpensive, and make nice aviary birds.

CHAPTER XII.

THE QUAIL FAMILY
(*Phasianidæ*).

*The Californian Quail—The Coromandel Quail—
The Australian and Tasmanian Quails—The
Argoondah Quail.*

UAILS are members of the gallinaceous order, *Gallinæ*; but why they should have been included in the Pheasant family rather than in any other connected with it, does not to me appear very clear. However, there they are, and there I am fain to leave them—for the present at all events.

At first sight a Quail does not look a very likely subject to make a pet of, but a closer acquaintance with several of them proves to demonstration that there are few nicer birds to keep. In the first place, though naturally timid, they soon become familiar; secondly, some of them breed quite freely in confinement, and the young, when properly treated, are not more difficult to rear than chickens; and thirdly, they are by no means difficult to preserve in health and condition.

THE CALIFORNIAN QUAIL, *Callipepla californica*, is a most delightful bird, with but one drawback that I know of, namely, a somewhat "touchy" disposition. It is a plump, well-proportioned bird, not quite as big as a partridge, of which it has very much the carriage. The distinguishing feature of the species consists in a tuft of plumes—black in the male and dark grey in the female—that ornaments the head. The whole of the plumage is dark chocolate-brown, except the abdomen and under-tail coverts, which are nearly white. A crescent-shaped white stripe extends backwards from the eyes for half an inch, and another white stripe starts from the base of the upper mandible and passes in a circle round the throat. I do not know of any birds that become so thoroughly tame with their owner as these very charming Quails—so tame indeed as to be almost a nuisance; while their pretty plumage and quaint cries combine to make them the most delightful of pets. They cannot, however, be kept with other poultry, and must have an enclosure to themselves, which, however, they will share with thrushes, parrakeets, and other feathered fowl of that kind, without any interference. It is only gallinaceous birds that they evince any objection to.

The eggs, which vary from ten to twenty in number, are creamy white, spotted and blotched with chestnut-brown; they differ greatly in appearance, however, and I have seen some almost white. Incubation lasts twenty-one days, and the young run about directly they leave the shell. They may be reared quite readily on ants' eggs (as bought), a custard made with egg and milk, fine oatmeal, gentles well scoured in bran, chopped lettuce, and a little hard-boiled yolk of fresh eggs. As they get older they should be gradually accustomed to a diet of millet and corn.

THE COROMANDEL QUAIL, *Coturnix coromandelica,* is a charming little species from India, and is about the size of our English Quail, to which it bears considerable resemblance, though it is a trifle larger, and has a black, shield-like spot on the breast. The female lacks this distinctive mark.

THE AUSTRALIAN and TASMANIAN QUAILS, *Synæcus australis* and *Synæcus diemenensis*, two nearly allied species, breed in confinement almost as readily as the Californian.

THE ARGOONDAH QUAIL, a native of Southern India, another free breeder, must close my list, which would not be exhausted if I were to enumerate twenty species more. The scientific name of the last mentioned is *Coturnix argoondah* (Russ) or *asiatica;* it is of a brownish colour above, and black and white disposed in narrow, alternate lines on the lower part of the body.

All the Quails incubate for twenty-one days, and should be fed on small corn, canary, millet, dari, &c., with green food, and an occasional feed of ants' eggs or gentles.

CHAPTER XIII.

THE ROBIN FAMILY
(*Motacillidæ*).

The Blue Robin—The Pekin Robin—The Australian Robin.

OBINS are pretty widely distributed, and representatives of the family are to be met with nearly everywhere, though they differ a good deal from each other in size, colour, and habits.

THE BLUE ROBIN, *Sialia wilsonii* (illustrated at Fig. 23), is a very handsome bird from North America. It is somewhat larger than our familiar redbreast. All the upper parts of the body of the male are dark sky-blue, the breast and under-surface reddish-brown, except the vent, which is white; the female is smaller, and her blue coat is shaded with grey.

These birds frequently breed in confinement, but do not always rear the young. The proper food is ants' eggs, mealworms, insects of all kinds, and bread and milk, or custard made of egg and milk, a little raw meat occasionally, and the yolk of hard-boiled egg.

THE PEKIN ROBIN, *Liothrix luteus*, figures at the "Zoo" among the tits, but may quite as well be included in the present family. It is too well known to need description, and should be treated as recommended for the previous species, than which it is a little smaller. Male and female are alike; but the colours of the latter are duller, and she does not sing.

THE AUSTRALIAN ROBIN, *Motacilla australis*, is a very handsome little bird, black on the upper parts,

FIG. 23. THE BLUE ROBIN.

with a carmine breast and white under-parts. It is tolerably abundant in the bush, where I have frequently listened to its short though very agreeable song; but I have never seen any of them in this country, and do not think any have been imported, though they might be kept readily enough on the diet recommended above.

Many dealers advise millet for the Robins, but they soon die of it—in fits.

CHAPTER XIV.

THE SPARROW FAMILY

(*Passeridæ*).

The Saffron Sparrow—The Red-throated Sparrow
The Java Sparrow—The Diamond Sparrow—The
Parson "Finch"—The Zebra or Chestnut-eared
"Finch"—The Double-banded, Gould's, and the
Painted "Finches."

PARROWS, as a rule, are grouped with
the Finches, from which they differ in
many material points; they are a
numerous family, and I can only make a
selection from among them.

THE SAFFRON SPARROW, commonly called SAFFRON
FINCH, *Sycalis flaveola*, is a well-known species, and
a favourite with amateurs, in consequence of its breeding freely in confinement. The male is a bright,
greenish-yellow, except on the head, which is deep
saffron colour; the female is much greyer, and can
be readily distinguished when the sexes are seen
together. The young all resemble her, and the
males cannot be told with certainty until they moult.

Millet and canary-seed form the diet of these birds.

which make a nest of hay, lined with feathers, in any convenient hollow, and lay from three to five white eggs, thickly streaked with blackish-grey. There are two or three broods in the season, and when young ones are in the nest, ants' eggs and soaked bread, with or without milk, must be added to the bill of fare. Habitat, Brazil.

Attempts to produce mules with the canary have resulted in complete failure.

THE RED-THROATED SPARROW, or CORAL or RIBBON FINCH, *Amadina fasciata* (illustrated at

FIG. 24. THE RED-THROATED SPARROW.

Fig. 24), is a well-known species, conspicuous by a red mark across the throat of the male, to which it owes the ominous appellation (Cut-throat) by which it is generally known.

Food and treatment as in the case of the preceding species.

THE JAVA SPARROW, *Padda oryzivora* (illustrated at Fig. 25), is another well-known bird, of which there are two distinct varieties—the ordinary leaden-blue and the white, both of which breed quite freely

in the aviary, where they will rear numerous broods
without fuss or trouble on the diet recommended
above.

FIG. 25.   THE JAVA SPARROW.

THE DIAMOND SPARROW, *Amadina lathami* (see
Fig. 26), is an Australian species frequently imported,
but not so free a breeder in confinement as any of
the preceding.   It is a pretty bird, with a melancholy,

FIG. 26.   THE DIAMOND SPARROW.

wailing cry, makes a large nest of grass, snugly lined
with feathers, in a tall bush or in a cage or box, lays
four or five white eggs, and feeds its young on a
combined diet of seed and insects.

THE PARSON "FINCH," *Poëphila cincta,* is a native
of the eastern parts of Australia, and bears many
points of resemblance to the preceding, but is altogether a more striking-looking bird; it is a trifle
smaller than the Diamond Sparrow, which about equals
our siskin in size. The general colour is brown, the
head and neck are bluish-grey, a black band crosses
the throat and another passes behind the thighs; the
under-tail coverts are white, and the tail black.

Food and treatment the same as recommended for
the last species.

FIG. 27.   THE ZEBRA FINCH.

THE ZEBRA or CHESTNUT-EARED "FINCH," *Amadina
castanotis* (illustrated at Fig. 27), is rather smaller than
the preceding, but, like it, a true Sparrow and a native
of Eastern Australia.

The male is a perky little creature somewhat difficult
to describe; the female is readily distinguished from
her mate by the absence of purple-spotted sides and
the chestnut-coloured ear patches, her plumage being
for the most part grey; the beak is coral-red. The
young resemble the hen, but have a black instead of

a red bill. Treatment and food identical with the previous species.

It breeds very freely in captivity, producing from three to seven young four or five times a year.

THE DOUBLE-BANDED, GOULD'S, and the PAINTED "FINCHES" can only be mentioned; the two last are rare and consequently expensive, delicate, and quite out of reach of the ordinary amateur.

The remaining members of the family, which are many, cannot even be named within the limits of this work.

CHAPTER XV.

THE STARLING FAMILY
(*Sturnidæ*).

The Glossy Starlings—Mynahs—The Rose-coloured Pastor.

HIS is a well-defined family, or "natural order," and comprises some very noticeable birds, foremost among which are THE GLOSSY STARLINGS, Genus *Lamprocolius,* namely, THE GREEN GLOSSY STARLING, *L. chalybeus;* THE PURPLE-HEADED GLOSSY STARLING, *L. auratus;* THE RUFOUS-VENTED GLOSSY STARLING, *L. rufiventris;* and THE LONG-TAILED GLOSSY STARLING, *Lamprotornis æneus,* all magnificent creatures, glistening in the sunshine with metallic hues of green, bronze, gold, and purple. Many of them have bred in confinement, and all require the same treatment as our English Starling: namely, meat, insects, egg, fruit, and custard, though many other things may be added to eke out the above.

THE MYNAHS, Genus *Gracula,* are included in this family, and some of them make splendid talkers and mimics; their general colour is black, with yellow beaks and legs, but THE MALABAR MYNAH, *Sturnia malabarica*, is grey and brown. It has nested in confinement in more than one aviary, but is rather quarrelsome during the breeding season.

THE ROSE-COLOURED PASTOR, *Pastor roseus*, is a Starling with a light pink breast and a black crest; its habitat is India, but not infrequently it makes migratory incursions into Central Europe, and has even, it is said, occasionally visited our shores; but I fancy the two or three specimens that have been shot here had escaped from aviaries, and were not emigrants of their own free will and accord.

It requires the same treatment as our native representative of the family.

CHAPTER XVI.

THE TANAGER FAMILY
(*Tanagridæ*).

The Superb Tanager—The Brazilian Tanager—The Violet Tanager—The All-Green Tanager—The Thick-billed Tanager—The Black-headed Tanager —The Green-headed Tanager, &c.

HIS family includes some of the very handsomest birds that are to be met with in any part of the world, but, except the species described in this chapter, are seldom imported, as they are difficult to preserve alive in confinement.

THE SUPERB TANAGER, *Calliste fastuosa*, is a bird that almost beggars description, so many and varied are the hues of its brilliant coat, on which bluish-green with a golden gloss vies with velvety black, and golden orange with pale blue, and the deepest azure, all combining to produce a *tout-ensemble* that might well be taken for a creature of the artist's imagination had not many specimens of the bird been seen alive at various times in the collection of the Zoological Society, and even in those of amateurs, while scarcely a show takes place at the Crystal Palace without one or more Superb Tanagers being exhibited. The size of this brilliant creature is about that of our goldfinch. It is unfortunate that so gorgeous a denizen of the tropics should be short-lived in our bleak climate, but so it is, in spite of infinite care, even at the "Zoo." The food should · consist almost entirely of ripe grapes and ants' eggs.

THE BRAZILIAN TANAGER, *Ramphocœlus brasilius* (illustrated at Fig. 28), is a much larger, if less showy,

FIG. 28. THE BRAZILIAN TANAGER.

bird than the last, being about the size of a lark. It is of a rich purple-red colour all over, except the wings and tail, which are jet black. The female is reddish-brown, with a deeper shade of brown on the wings. This species has been bred repeatedly, and the young reared successfully, by a lady aviarist in Belgium, but not as yet, that I have heard, elsewhere. The food is raw beef, shredded up fine; boiled rice, sweetened; grapes, oranges, raisins, and ants' eggs.

G

THE VIOLET TANAGER, *Euphonia violacea*, is one of the small species, not exceeding the siskin in size. On the back it is of a dark violet-black, and on the lower parts a rich yellow. It is frequently imported, but never endures very long unless supplied with plenty of sweet fruit: grapes, pears, oranges, bananas, and so on. It is a quiet little bird, which is more than can be said of the Brazilian Tanager.

Other members of the family, or group, are THE ALL-GREEN TANAGER, *Chlorophonia viridis*, sufficiently described by its name; THE THICK-BILLED TANAGER, *Euphonia crassirostris;* THE BLACK-HEADED TANAGER, *Pipridea melanonota;* THE GREEN-HEADED TANAGER, *Calliste tricolor*, and THE FESTIVE TANAGER, *Calliste festiva*—all fine birds, and named, except the last, from some distinguishing characteristic of form or colouring.

CHAPTER XVII.

THE THRUSH FAMILY
(*Turdidæ*).

The American Mocking-Bird—The American Robin— The Rock Thrush—The Blue or Solitary Thrush — The Grey-winged Blackbird — The Orange- headed Ground Thrush—The Sorry Thrush—The Brown Thrush.

EPRESENTATIVES of the Thrush family are to be met with in all parts of the globe, from the Falkland Islands in the Southern to Iceland in the Northern Atlantic, as well as in every intermediate station, both in the Old World and the New.

THE AMERICAN MOCKING-BIRD, *Mimus polyglottus* (see Fig. 29), perhaps the most famous member of the family, and concerning which so much has been written by Wilson, Audubon, and other American naturalists, is an insignificant-looking grey bird, less in size than our Thrush and of slimmer build; its lower parts are greyish-white. The female greatly resembles the male, and has frequently bred in confinement in this country. As the Mocking-Bird I had in my

possession some years ago never sang, it was probably
a female. The food is similar to that provided for

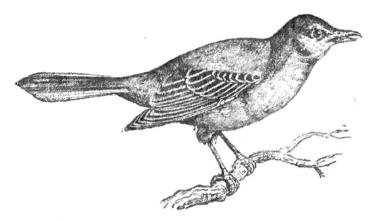

FIG. 29. THE AMERICAN MOCKING-BIRD.

larks, but more ants' eggs should be given, and occasionally a little raw lean meat.

THE AMERICAN ROBIN, *Turdus migratorius*, is a

FIG. 30. THE ROCK THRUSH.

Thrush, and derives its English name from its ruddy
breast.

THE ROCK THRUSH, *Monticola saxatilis* (illustrated

at Fig. 30), is a small bird, with the head, neck, and back of a deep bluish-grey, the shoulders blackish, the lower part of the back and the rump white, the upper tail-coverts and the tail itself red, the wings dark brown, each feather marked with a small darker spot of the same colour, the under-parts reddish-brown, the irides brown, and the bill blue-grey. The female is duller in appearance, and has the tail and tail-coverts reddish-brown.

FIG. 31. THE BLUE THRUSH.

Nearly all authorities are agreed as to the merits of the Rock Thrush as a songster, but it is not a common bird, and consequently commands a high price. It should be fed as advised for the American Mocking-Bird. Habitat, Central Europe.

THE BLUE or SOLITARY THRUSH, *Monticola cyanus* (illustrated at Fig. 31), is even more seldom met with than the preceding, which it fairly rivals in personal beauty and vocal merits. The upper parts are dark bluish-grey, but the head and back are sky-blue; the wings and tail are bluish-black, the eyes brown, and the legs and feet black.

The food should be identical with that recommended for the preceding species, than which it is even more expensive in this country. Habitat, Central Europe.

Other members of the family, all exceedingly desirable as inmates of the soft-billed birds' aviary, are THE GREY-WINGED BLACKBIRD, *Turdus pœcilopterus*, from Cashmere; THE ORANGE-HEADED GROUND THRUSH, *Geocichla citrina;* THE SORRY THRUSH, *T. tristis*, from Mexico; and THE BROWN THRUSH, *T. leucomelas*, from South America.

CHAPTER XVIII.

THE WARBLER FAMILY
(*Sylviidæ*).

The Nonpareil—The Pin-tail or East Indian Nonpareil—The Indian Dial-Bird, or Shamah.

ARBLERS are a well-defined group, and I may be straining relationships a trifle when I include with them such birds as the Nonpareils and the Indigo Warbler; but I do not see where else I can put the latter, unless I take him as the type of a distinct family, which I scarcely think I should be warranted in doing.

THE NONPAREIL, *Cyanospiza ciris*, is a well-known bird whose chief habitat is in the southern parts of the United States, whence it is annually exported to Europe in very large numbers, which, as a rule, soon die in consequence of the general ignorance that prevails as to its habits and position in the great family of birds.

Few of our foreign favourites are more brilliantly clad than the Nonpareil, with his head, neck, and throat shimmering with bright violet-blue tints; his wings of reddish-brown; back, shoulders, and edges of the tail feathers yellowish-green, while the rest of the under-parts are scarlet.

The female is much more soberly attired in yellowish-green, and the young males resemble her; so that amateurs who think they have a pair are very often disappointed when they find they have only got an old cock and a young one.

These birds have occasionally bred in confinement, making a nest of hay or fibre in a bush on a foundation of their own construction, or in a basket hung up behind some convenient shelter. The eggs, which are from three to five in number, are bluish-white, speckled with violet and brown. The readiest food consists of ants' eggs, given as bought, and to this should be added small ripe fruit, gentles in the pupa stage of their existence, groats, and millet. It must be recollected that these birds are mainly insectivorous, and cannot live long on a diet composed of seed alone, which they cannot digest in any quantity, and which if persisted in will cause constipation and fits, from which so many Nonpareils die in captivity.

THE PIN-TAIL or EAST INDIAN NONPAREIL, *Erythrura prasina,* is a native of Java and Sumatra, and at one time used to be very freely imported; but, owing to its correct management not being understood, it seldom survived long in this country, and amateurs gave it up. However, it may be preserved as long as its American cousin, by adopting for it the dietary recommended for the latter, with the addition of a free supply of paddy rice; that is to say, rice in the husk, on which it has even bred in the aviary of Dr. Russ, of Berlin.

The arrangement of colours in the Pin-tail Nonpareil is very similar to that in the American bird, although they are scarcely as intense as in the latter; the tail feathers, however, are brown with scarlet edges, but the central pair are much longer than the others, and terminate in a fine point, whence the name; they are dark scarlet in colour.

The female is olive-green on the back, dull yellowish-brown underneath, and wants the blue head and scarlet belly.

Size about that of our goldfinch.

THE INDIAN DIAL-BIRD, or SHAMAH, *Copsychus saularis*, which, notwithstanding its first English name, is found in the southern parts of China and the Philippine Islands, as well as in India, is everywhere highly esteemed as a songster and a very charming cage pet.

It is a slim-made bird, very light and graceful in its movements, and although expensive, very frequently to be seen at shows, where it generally commands attention.

In size it is somewhat less than an English thrush, and requires feeding as recommended on a previous page for the mocking-bird.

It has bred repeatedly in the western aviary at the "Zoo," and would doubtless do so in private aviaries if females could be more readily obtained; these are very seldom imported, however, and appear to be more delicate in confinement than their mates.

Mr. R. Phillipps, to whom I am indebted for particulars of the Scops Owl and the Drongo, has kindly supplied the following account of the Shâmah, which from personal experience he can strongly recommend as making, in good hands, a most interesting pet. He says:—" The Shâmah is a little larger and longer than the nightingale, with a longer tail, and is like to that bird in many of its habits. At first sight it appears to be black over all the upper parts, and also on the head, neck, throat, and upper part of breast. The flight feathers are, however, brown of different shades, and the feathers on the lower part of the back are white. The centre four feathers of the tail are longer than the others, and of a dead-black colour ; the four feathers on either side being black with white ends ; the outer feathers having more white than the inner, the line between the two colours being drawn slanting. The black feathers entirely conceal the white below, so that when the bird is crouching in a dark corner, as it habitually does when frightened, not a speck of white shows, and the bird is almost invisible, except to a practised eye. When flying, however, the white is conspicuous. On rare occasions, when excited by the presence of a rival, and probably also when courting, the male moves the white feathers of the tail scissors fashion, with great rapidity, producing a curious effect. The lower part of the breast, the under-parts, and the small feathers under the shoulders, are of a rich reddish-brown, the line between this colour and the black on the upper part of the breast being sharply drawn. In the male, the black of the head, neck, and shoulders is very deep and glossy. In the female, however, these parts are more slate-coloured, and the colours generally less distinct. The wings are rounded, the fourth feather being the longest, and the flight is jerky and rather weak. The legs and claws are dull white, the beak black-brown. The total length of an ordinary male is 10in., of which the tail is 5¾in.

"The Shâmah delights in dark holes and corners, and when in the garden usually keeps low down among the shrubs and thickets. It is exceedingly fond of the lower and smaller boughs of rhododendron bushes, and from the midst of these will warble forth its sweet and gentle song by the hour, ascending and hiding among the leaves at roosting-time. So low and gentle is this song that it can be heard only by those who are near, and by those who have observant ears. Some people seldom hear the voice of the charmer, charm he never so wisely. In the house during the winter also the Shâmah gives forth its sweetest strains when entirely hidden from view in some dark corner. What a sweet-tempered, gentle, amiable, little darling! So you may say if you have but one. Alas! our sweet-tempered angel has but to hear a note from one of its kind when, emerging from its obscurity and casting all its amiability to the winds, bounding to the top of the highest available post of observation, it pours forth such a volley of abuse, in notes of defiance so powerful and full, that it is difficult to believe that it is the same bird, or sometimes, indeed, that such notes can come from a bird at all. If the intruder be "get-at-able," a chase immediately follows, and the stranger will probably be injured or destroyed unless the birds be separated. For a time I

kept two fairly-matched males in my garden, in the
non-rapacious birds' aviary ; but it was a mistake.
It was worth a king's ransom, nevertheless, to see
them, from time to time, on the ground, face to face,
a few inches apart, singing, whistling, and warbling
at one another, in notes which were perfectly
marvellous, and far excelling anything I have ever
heard coming from a lone bird.   Undoubtedly the
Shâmah is a wondrous songster and whistler ; but
individual specimens vary considerably, probably according to their bringing up.   I have been told of
a Shâmah which could whistle several tunes with
perfect accuracy.   This bird died eventually of old
age, having been in the same home for a number
of years.   The ordinary call-notes of the Shâmah,
however, are repeated too frequently by some specimens, until they become monotonous.

"It is not seen to advantage when kept shut up in
a cage.   Like the nightingale—and many owners of
nightingales do not know this—if allowed plenty of
liberty, it will become very bold, familiar, and tame,
taking food freely from the hand.   In the house it
should have a cage for its home, in which its food,
&c., should be placed—a cage with an open door.
One I had in my dining-room used to come on to the
table at meal-times, take pieces of meat off my plate,
and hop about quite at home ; and it would retire to
its den and warble forth a song of thankfulness and
praise, putting many of the lords of creation to shame.
The same with one in my bird-room, or in the garden
during the summer, always popping out from somewhere with a 'Tit,' and an impudent jerk of the tail,

on the look-out for a mealworm. And this 'popping out from somewhere,' or often from 'nowhere,' is one of the idiosyncrasies of the bird. The door may have been left open, and the Shâmah has disappeared. You may search every nook and corner, high and low, upstairs and downstairs, but no Shâmah. You come into the room an hour later, and there is your bird all right

"If confined in a cage, it should be in a box-cage, or in one which has a sheltered and darkened corner, and in the cage there should be a small natural bough, and also a ledge or box high up, as it is very fond of roosting on a flat place and high.

"The Shâmah will thrive much better in a garden aviary during the summer than in the house, especially if there be plenty of shrubs and places of shelter. Indeed, if confined in a cage in the house during the warm weather, it is apt to pluck out its feathers, unless fed with tiresome judiciousness. It is best to bring it back to the house as soon as it shows signs of moulting, as it will throw out a much finer tail in the warm than in the cold. But, although bearing a good deal of cold, if sudden changes of temperature be avoided, it is a delicate bird in another way. It is nervous, excitable, and naturally timid; and if it be confined in an open cage without a dark retreat, or with too large perches, you may expect a paralytic seizure. It must have a supply of good grit, plenty of water for both drinking and washing, and doughy and indigestible food must be avoided like poison. It is very keen after mealworms, cockroaches, and insects of all kinds. The more small insects you can place in its way, the better; and for stock food, the same as that given to nightingales will suit. Two males should not be kept together, and even towards nightingales, blue robins, and some other soft-billed birds, it is not always too friendly. But in my garden, where there is plenty of cover and a good deal of space, I have never known the Shâmah interfere with any bird but one of its own species."

CHAPTER XIX.

THE WAXBILL FAMILY
(*Æginthidæ*).

The Grey or Common Waxbill—The St. Helena Waxbill—The Orange-cheeked Waxbill—The Cinereous Waxbill—The Crimson-eared Waxbill—The Avadavat Waxbill—The Green Waxbill—The Golden-breasted Waxbill—The Red African Waxbill—The Violet-eared Waxbill — The Sydney or Australian Waxbill.

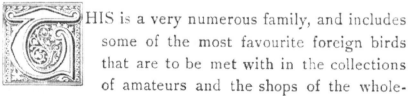THIS is a very numerous family, and includes some of the most favourite foreign birds that are to be met with in the collections of amateurs and the shops of the whole-sale importers and dealers in this country. They are tiny birds for the most part, with pretty plumage and lively ways, but little or no power of song. They are easily kept in confinement, being very frugal livers, subsisting for the most part on white sorghum- (millet) seed, and not infrequently nesting in the aviary with as much readiness and more success than the canary.

THE GREY or COMMON WAXBILL, *Estrelda* (or *Ægintha*, Russ) *cinerea* (illustrated at Fig. 32), is a

charming little creature, not much bigger than a
golden-crested wren. It is a native of Eastern Africa,
but has been naturalised at St. Helena and in other
places, and is imported by thousands into this country.
The colour of this miniature bird is grey, darker on
the upper than on the lower parts of the body, which
last are suffused with a subdued rosy tint, deepening
at the vent; the feathers of the back, back of the
neck, and head are marked with wavy lines of a
darker shade than the body colour; the bill is bright

FIG. 32. THE GREY WAXBILL.

red, and a streak of the same colour passes from it
across the face, embracing the eyes, and terminating
beyond the ears; the legs and feet are grey, and the
tail feathers, except the central pair, which are dark
brown, are edged with white.

In confinement these tiny creatures make a big
nest of fibre or hay snugly lined with feathers, either
in a bush or the centre of a birch-broom; or they
will avail themselves of the convenience and protection
of a Hartz-Mountain canary-cage. The eggs are pure

white, five or six in number, and about the size of a
pea; the young are hatched in eleven or twelve days,
and are readily enough reared on ants' eggs and
aphides, both of which should be freely supplied to
the parents. On emerging from the nest, the young
ones are all grey, and have black bills.

THE ST. HELENA WAXBILL, *Estrelda rubriventris*
(see Fig 33), is sometimes absurdly called the Pheasant
Finch. It is a larger bird than the preceding, to
which, however, it bears a general resemblance, and,

FIG. 33. THE ST. HELENA WAXBILL.

like it, though a native of the eastern parts of Africa,
has become established at St. Helena in such numbers
that it does serious damage to the millet crops, and
is caught in thousands, which are exported to Europe
and America, where it is in much request as a handsome, hardy, and lively inmate of the parlour aviary.

The wavy lines on the back and sides of this
species are much more pronounced than in the case
of the Grey Waxbill; the under-parts, especially the

H

vent, are of a much deeper red, and the red of the bill and eye-streak more intense. The long tail is black and kept in incessant motion, now jerked up and down, then spread out fan-wise; and whether the bird is feeding, hopping about, or singing, the tail vibrates in keeping with every movement, and has been compared, not inaptly, to the pendulum of a clock.

This pretty bird not only breeds freely with members of its own species in the aviary, but will also pair and produce hybrids with the Grey Waxbill, as well as contract matrimonial alliances with the members of other species — which, however, I have found to be unfruitful. For instance, a male that has been in my possession for several years paired last summer (1890) with a hen canary, but the only result was barren eggs, though the little Waxbill was most attentive to his yellow-coated spouse.

The food, treatment, and nesting arrangements of this species are identical with those of the last.

THE ORANGE-CHEEKED WAXBILL, *Estrelda melpoda* (illustrated at Fig. 34), is another charming species, the same size as the Grey Waxbill; its general colour is brown on the upper and greyish-white on the under-parts of the body; the rump is red, and the tail nearly black; a reddish-orange patch surrounds the eye, the beak is of the same colour, and the legs and feet of a reddish flesh-tint.

It is an exceedingly free breeder in the aviary. One that I had for a long time paired with a hen Cordon Bleu, and the eggs were fertile; but an accident overtook them just as they were due to hatch, and the chance did not occur again.

The food and treatment of this species are the same as in the case of those preceding. Many readers will, no doubt, seeing that all these birds are of African origin, be surprised to hear that they are so hardy that they will even bear to be wintered out of doors with impunity in this bleak climate of ours. They must, however, of course have a snug aviary, well protected from the weather, and especially from the rain, which is far more fatal to them than the cold. They must also have cosy nests, in which to

FIG. 34. THE ORANGE-CHEEKED WAXBILL.

pass the long, weary hours of darkness; and, above all, there must be no mice about to drive them out of their comfortable sleeping places in the night, to perish from fright and cold before morning.

THE CINEREOUS WAXBILL, *Estrelda cærulescens*, also called the Lavender Finch, is another West African species, about the same size as the last. The general colour is a delicate lavender-grey, deeper on the back, wings, and shoulders than on the breast and belly. The rump and tail are bright red, and the feathers of the vent and the under-tail coverts dusky red; the bill is dark red, and the eye-streak black; the legs and feet are grey.

This species is more delicate than the preceding, and is decidedly impatient of cold. It is a troublesome little bird, too, in the aviary, from a habit it has of plucking its companions; for which reason I am not as well acquainted with its habits as with those of the birds I have already described, nor has it ever bred with me. Food: millet- and canary-seed.

THE CRIMSON-EARED WAXBILL, commonly known as THE CORDON BLEU, *Estrelda phænicotis*, is decidedly one of the nicest birds out. It had at one time the reputation of being very delicate, and for a long time I entertained the same opinion; but further experience with it convinced me at last that this was quite a mistake, and that the Cordon Bleu was not less tender than its congeners.

It is an excessively pretty little creature, the same size as those previously noticed (except the St. Helena), and may thus be described: bill, red; face, breast, sides, tail, light blue; top of head, neck, back, and wings, ash-grey; ear-coverts, crimson; legs and feet, pale flesh-colour.

The female resembles her mate, but wants the crimson ear-patch, and is very pretty and gentle; she breeds quite freely in the aviary, and if she cannot find a mate of her own species, will take up with any of the preceding. The young on emerging from the nest resemble their mother, but have black bills.

Food, &c., as for the preceding species.

THE AVADAVAT WAXBILL, *Estrelda amandava* (illustrated at Fig. 35), is a common Indian bird, also known as the Tiger Finch. It is about the same size as the Grey Waxbill, but is subject to numerous changes of plumage, not only at different ages, but at different seasons of the year. It is decidedly a more delicate creature than the African Waxbills, but should be fed and treated as advised for them.

When in full plumage the male is a handsome little fellow, resplendent in bronze and gold, and plentifully speckled with white spots; the female is grey, and

FIG. 35. THE AVADAVAT WAXBILL.

does not change colour, but when the male is in undress he resembles his partner in a general way, only that his costume is a trifle darker than hers.

One great drawback these little birds have—namely, they are very apt to become bald and otherwise featherless; and when this happens, I have never known the plumage to be reproduced.

Some I had for a long time used to build nests freely, but never laid, and I believe it is very rare for the Avadavat to breed in this country.

THE GREEN WAXBILL, or GREEN AVADAVAT, *Estrelda formosa*, which is a pretty bird, is somewhat larger than the common Avadavat. The upper parts of the body are dark olive-green; the wings and tail dark greenish-brown; the lower parts are dull yellow, all more or less marked with wavy lines of a darker shade than the body colours; the beak is bright red. There is very little difference between the sexes, but the colours of the female are duller than those of the male.

Though common in their own country—India—they are not very frequently imported. I have not heard of their breeding in this country, and I have found them decidedly delicate.

Food and treatment the same as for the other Waxbills.

THE GOLDEN-BREASTED WAXBILL, *Estrelda subflava*, is the least of all the Waxbills, and is as pretty as it is small, and otherwise desirable.

The upper part of the body is dark olivaceous-brown; the wings and the tail dark greenish-brown; the lower parts are golden-yellow, with a reddish tinge on the breast and at the vent; the sides are darker, and each tiny feather in that situation has a yellow edge; the beak is dusky red, and a line of dark orange surmounts the eye like an eyebrow.

The female is altogether duskier in appearance, and lacks the golden sheen on the breast; but her sides present the same zebra markings as her mate—markings to which these diminutive creatures owe another of their names: that of Zebra Waxbill.

Their food and mode of nesting are exactly like that

of their congeners, but the eggs are the smallest I ever saw, with the exception of some almost microscopical specimens laid by humming-birds.

In my aviary these very charming little creatures have frequently built nests and laid eggs; but, owing to one mischance or another, never succeeded in producing any young. Other amateurs, however, have been more fortunate. Dr. Russ relates an instance in which a pair of these birds brought up no less than fifty-four young ones in one year out of 121 eggs laid by the same hen.

THE RED AFRICAN WAXBILL, also known as THE FIRE FINCH, *Estrelda minima*, is about the same size as the preceding species. The head, neck, breast, and rump are vivid scarlet; the back and wings reddish-brown; the vent olivaceous-brown, and the lower two-thirds of the tail dark brown; the bill is red, and the legs and feet are bright flesh-colour. The female is greyish-brown, with a subtint of red where that colour predominates in the male; her beak is a paler red than his, but her legs and feet rather darker.

This tiny bird will breed freely in confinement if kept comfortably warm, but will not do so if the temperature of the place where he is kept falls much below 70deg. Fahr., while 80deg. or 90deg. will also suit him very well. He would be quite at home in a hot-house, where he would keep the plants clear of insects, and do no harm himself; while the small amount of dirt he and his partner would make could readily be got rid of by the syringe.

Food and treatment (except warmth), the same as for the other Waxbills.

THE VIOLET-EARED WAXBILL, *Estrelda granatica*, is as rare in this country as the last species is common. It is a native of the same parts of Africa—namely West and Central—but is much hardier than the Red Waxbill. The general colour is a rich, soft brown, a narrow rim of very bright blue encircles the beak, and another the root of the tail, the cheeks are marked by a large patch of brilliant violet, and the beak is coral-red.

The female is generally duller in appearance than her mate, and her cheeks show less of the distinctive violet colouring than his.

Both sexes, but especially the male, sing very sweetly. So far, I have not heard of their breeding in confinement.

Food: millet- and a little canary-seed, ants' eggs, crumbled sponge-cake, and a few small mealworms daily.

THE SYDNEY or AUSTRALIAN WAXBILL, *Estrelda temporalis*, is a common bird in its native land, but is nevertheless not of such frequent occurrence here as many of its congeners, in consequence of its being generally thought delicate: I have not found it so— at least, not more delicate than the other Waxbills; and Dr. Russ has succeeded more than once in getting them to breed in his aviary.

The top of the head, back of the neck, back, and wings are olive-green; the throat and face greenish-blue; the breast and belly yellowish-green; the tail very dark green; the beak is bright red, and a broad streak of the same colour passes from it, surrounding the eye, to the back of the head: the rump and upper tail-coverts are also bright red; the legs and feet are yellowish-grey.

The female is like her mate, but has a somewhat smaller eye-mark. They are very peaceable and quiet little birds, about the size of the Green Waxbill, and require to be fed and treated in the same way.

CHAPTER XX.

THE WEAVER FAMILY.
(*Ploceidæ*).

The Napoleon Weaver — The Yellow-shouldered Weaver — The Crimson-crowned Weaver — The Oryx Weaver—The Red-headed or Madagascar Weaver—The Orange Weaver, or Orange Bishop—The Red-headed Weaver — The Black-faced Weaver, or Red-beaked Weaver—The Paradise Whydah—The Pin-tailed Whydah—The Yellow-backed Whydah—The Combassou.

THIS very curious group of birds is confined to the great African Continent, and numbers in its ranks many beautiful and desirable species. They are chiefly characterised by their habit of weaving nests of such surpassing strength and beauty of construction as to be unequalled by any other members of the class Aves in this respect; another of their peculiarities being that the males, just before the season of pairing, or rather at its commencement, make what are called "toy nests;" that is to say, artistic constructions of no apparent use, seeing that they are not even occupied for sleeping purposes, and differ considerably in shape from the nests proper built by the females for the reception of their eggs and young. The materials used in both cases consist of tough grass stems, so firmly interwoven that they cannot be pulled asunder without difficulty.

Many of these birds have bred in confinement, and the males are always ready to show off their skill at toy-nest building ; and these cleverly-woven bowers, which the architects themselves make no use of, are very serviceable as sleeping boxes for the Waxbills and other tiny people of that sort.

THE NAPOLEON WEAVER, *Ploceus melanogaster* (Russ), is a curious-looking bird whose colours of brown, black, and yellow are disposed in the following manner: the top of the head, upper part of the neck, breast and sides, are bright yellow; the wings and tail are brown, each feather in the former having a darker edging; the throat, front of the face, lower part of the back of the neck, and the belly, velvety-black; the beak is white, and the strong legs and feet flesh-colour.

The female is brown; and when out of colour the male can only be distinguished from her by his somewhat larger size.

All the Weavers are hardy birds, change their plumage twice a year, and are fed on canary-seed and millet. They are very active, and should have plenty of room they do very well in an out-door aviary during the summer, but suffer from cold and damp, and should always be taken in during the inclement season.

At the London Zoological Gardens the Napoleon

Weaver is known by the name of *Euplectes afer*, and is classed with the Waxbills and Mannikins, which is confusing, and a little misleading too.

THE YELLOW-SHOULDERED WEAVER, *Euplectes capensis*, is a native of Tropical Africa, and must be treated accordingly. The general colour is black, but the shoulders and the middle of the back are bright yellow, the wings are greyish-brown.

THE CRIMSON-CROWNED WEAVER, *Euplectes flammiceps*, has the head, neck, throat, nape, breast and back, rump, and upper tail-coverts of scarlet; the shoulders are brown; the wings and tail black; the lores, ear-coverts, chin, lower breast, and belly black; the bill is also black.

The female is brown, and distinguishable from other female Weavers by the darker colour of her mandibles.

THE ORYX WEAVER, *Ploceus oryx* (Russ), or *Euplectes oryx*, is known in the trade as the Grenadier Weaver. It is just like a Napoleon Weaver whose yellow tints had been changed to a vivid red. The beak is dusky orange, and the legs and feet a brighter shade of the same colour. It is about the size of a well-grown goldfinch.

Writing of this bird, which he says breeds freely in the aviary, Mr. Wiener remarks: "One of the strangest sights a collection of Weaver-birds affords is the Oryx when endeavouring to attract the notice of the hen bird. He will gradually raise his body and blow himself out until he looks much larger than he is, and the feathers stand nearly erect; whilst he will utter sounds which seem a mixture of hissing, chirping, and the noise of scissors-grinding. Should the female remain indifferent to the charms of this music, he will chase her all over the aviary; but presently his vanity will overcome his wrath, and he will begin to blow himself out afresh."

THE RED-HEADED or MADAGASCAR WEAVER, *Foudia madagascariensis*, is a native of the island to which it owes its name (in the Zoological List it is said to come from the Isle of France); and, like many of its congeners, has become acclimatised in the Mauritius, at St. Helena, and elsewhere. It is a large bird, about the size of a common sparrow— all red, except the wings and tail, which are reddish-brown; the bill is white, and the legs and feet reddish-orange. In the aviary it is apt to be somewhat tyrannical, and should not be lodged with any of the Waxbills, whom it would probably harry to death during the breeding season, when it will also remorselessly persecute the smaller members of its own race.

Food and treatment as for the other Weavers.

THE ORANGE WEAVER, or ORANGE BISHOP, *Euplectes franciscanus*, is smaller than the last species, being about the size of a goldfinch. The male when in full colour is bright reddish-orange on the throat, upper part of breast, nape, shoulders, back, and the long upper tail-coverts; the top of the head is black, which is also the colour of the lower part of the breast and the belly; the beak is dusky red, and the legs and feet reddish.

It is an excitable and restless bird, and fights bitterly with the males of its own species; it does not even spare its own female, which it drives about incessantly during the breeding season. Still, as the Orange Bishop is an eminently handsome bird, many people will like to have it in their possession; and it is well they should be warned as to the character of the creature they are about to take to their bosoms. Notwithstanding, one male and one female of this species will do very well in a good-sized aviary placed entirely at their disposal, and in all probability will breed, if provided with suitable nesting-material and not unduly interfered with by the owner.

THE RED-HEADED WEAVER, *Foudia erythrops*, is distinguished by its bright red head, which curiously surmounts a brownish, sparrow-looking body. The beak is dusky horn-colour, and the legs and feet dull reddish-yellow.

THE BLACK-FACED WEAVER, or RED-BEAKED WEAVER, *Quelea sanguinirostris*, is a native of Western Africa, and is the most frequently imported of all the Weavers. It is one of the smallest members of its race. The bill is bright red, and is surrounded by a wide black ring; the rest of the head, neck, breast, and belly are reddish-yellowish-brown; the wings and tail are dark reddish-brown, and the legs and feet dull orange-colour.

There are quite a number of other Weaver-birds, but they are not 'as frequently imported as those I have named and described.

I now pass on to an allied group of birds which are usually classed with the Weavers, but nevertheless differ from them in many points, though they resemble them in others, and on the whole are better included in this family than placed in a division by themselves.

To English amateurs they are known as Whydah-birds, the name being derived from that part of the Dark Continent where most of them are to be met with—namely, the kingdom of Whydah on the West Coast of Africa, their distinguishing feature being the extraordinarily long tail grown by the male during the breeding season, when these elongated feathers frequently attain to a length of fourteen and even sixteen inches, which, as the bird itself only measures about five inches, is certainly a little out of proportion!

THE PARADISE WHYDAH, *Vidua paradisea* (illustrated at Fig. 36), is a most graceful creature. The general colour of the bird when in its full nuptial dress is black—that is to say, the head and face; the wings and the long tail are of that colour, but the neck, nape, and breast are dusky orange, while the belly and vent are a lighter shade of the same tint; the beak is dusky horn, and the legs and feet leaden-grey.

The tail consists of twelve feathers, the central pair of which grow to the greatest length and have an inward curve, so that when the tips nearly touch the ground as the bird hops about, the centre of these long plumes is a good way from it. The next pair are about a quarter of the length of the central pair and twice as broad—they are inserted sidewise, and have a hair-like termination which is really a prolongation of the midrib of the feather; the remaining tail feathers are short and inconspicuous.

These very handsome birds necessarily require a large cage, in order to preserve their strikingly-ornamental caudal appendage; and, placed in a large aviary, in perfect plumage, the graceful flight of the bird, with his long sweeping tail, is a sight of great

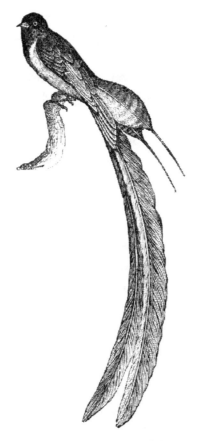

FIG. 36. THE PARADISE WHYDAH.

beauty. When feeding on the ground, the Whydah-bird carries his tail very carefully in a graceful curve, the tips of the long feathers just touching the ground, while the active feet scratch the sand, or mould, something after the fashion of the poultry tribe.

The long tail and the velvety-black plumage of the male are only worn for a short time; that is to say, during the breeding season: at other times it has a short tail and a greyish-brown coat, something like that of a caged redpoll—which is always that of the female; the latter, however, can be readily distinguished from her elegant husband by her much smaller size.

These birds are fed on millet- and canary-seed, but require the addition of ants' eggs during the moulting season.

It will be found to be a good plan to save the shells of all the eggs used in the house, dry them thoroughly in the oven or on top of the kitchen range, pound them up coarsely, and strew them on the floor of the aviary, where portions of them are greedily swallowed by all birds, the females elaborating from them shells for their own eggs, and both sexes finding help for the formation of their plumage from the carbonate of lime contained in the broken shells.

THE PIN-TAILED WHYDAH, *Vidua principalis* (illustrated at Fig. 37), is a smaller bird than the preceding, being about the size of a redpoll. Its tail is almost as long as that of the Paradise Whydah, but composed of much less conspicuous feathers, for they are not a third as broad as those of its congener. In young birds the elongated plumes number two only; but when the bird is three or four years old, they are increased to four.

The beak is red, a line round it is black, as are the head, nape, shoulders, back, and tail; the remaining portions of the plumage are white, except the large wing-coverts and the upper tail-coverts, which have a yellowish tinge.

The female is brownish-grey, but her beak resembles that of the male; the legs and feet of both sexes are lead-colour.

While the Paradise Whydah is a quiet, peaceable bird, the Pin-tail is a very quarrelsome and disagree-

FIG. 37. THE PIN-TAILED WHYDAH.

able inmate of the aviary, where he leads all the other birds a sad life, worrying and pursuing even those that are more than twice his size.

As in the case of the preceding species, the Pin-tailed Whydah only wears his distinctive garb during the breeding season, assuming at other times the appearance of the female.

It is said that this species has been bred in confinement; but the assertion is doubted by Mr. Wiener, nor have I seen any indication in specimens that have come under my notice at different times that would lead me to the conclusion that the Pin-tailed Whydah would be induced to nest and rear its brood in this country.

THE YELLOW-BACKED WHYDAH, *Coliopasser macrurus*, or, according to Dr. Russ, *Vidua macroura*, is a much larger bird than either of the preceding, attaining the size of a full-grown cock sparrow. It

FIG. 38. THE COMBASSOU.

is a very beautiful creature, clothed in velvety-black as to the greater portion of its plumage during the nuptial season, but the shoulders are golden yellow, and the centres of the wing-coverts a dark shade of the same colour; the bill is bluish-grey, the lower mandible being of a lighter tint than the upper; the legs and feet are dark lead-colour. The female is light grey on the back, with dark brown wings and tail. On the back and shoulders each feather has a narrow yellow edge, and the breast is greyish-white.

This species is of much rarer occurrence in this country than either of the preceding.

THE COMBASSOU, OR ULTRAMARINE FINCH, *Fringilla nitens* (illustrated at Fig. 38), is now generally allowed to be a member of the group we are considering. It is a very pretty little creature, quiet as a rule, but occasionally displaying a disposition to enact the part of tyrant over its companions, particularly during the breeding season, when it dons its beautiful steel-blue coat, for at other times it is not at all unlike a female redpoll.

This change of colour, and the habit of scratching with the feet on the ground, connect it clearly with the Whydahs, though it cannot boast of their excessive wealth of tail-feathering.

It is a native of Abyssinia, and requires to be kept warm, otherwise it will not moult, and will then soon fall into a decline.

Food. millet- and canary-seed, and ants' eggs, which must be given as bought.

Many more might be added to the foregoing did not exigencies of space forbid ; but it is hoped that the beautiful species here mentioned will suffice for beginners, at all events, who will find them the most charming and attractive of pets, and be well rewarded for the money, care, and attention spent upon the little strangers.

INDEX.

Catalogue of Practical Handbooks Published by L. Upcott Gill, 170, Strand, London, W.C.

ANGLER, BOOK OF THE ALL-ROUND. A Comprehensive Treatise on Angling in both Fresh and Salt Water. In Four Divisions, as named below. By JOHN BICKERDYKE. With over 220 Engravings. *In cloth, price 5s. 6d., by post 6s.* (A few copies of a LARGE PAPER EDITION, *bound in Roxburghe, price 25s.*)

Angling for Coarse Fish. Bottom Fishing, according to the Methods in use on the Thames, Trent, Norfolk Broads, and elsewhere. Illustrated. *In paper, price 1s., by post 1s. 2d.; cloth, 2s. (uncut), by post 2s. 3d.*

Angling for Pike. The most Approved Methods of Fishing for Pike or Jack. Profusely Illustrated. *In paper, price 1s., by post 1s. 2d.; cloth, 2s. (uncut), by post 2s. 3d.*

Angling for Game Fish. The Various Methods of Fishing for Salmon: Moorland, Chalk-stream, and Thames Trout; Grayling and Char. Well Illustrated. *In paper, price 1s. 6d., by post 1s. 9d.; cloth, 2s. 6d. (uncut), by post 2s 9d.*

Angling in Salt Water. Sea Fishing with Rod and Line, from the Shore, Piers, Jetties, Rocks, and from Boats; together with Some Account of Hand-Lining. Over 50 Engravings. *In paper, price 1s., by post 1s. 2d.; cloth, 2s. (uncut), by post 2s. 3d.*

AQUARIA, BOOK OF. A Practical Guide to the Construction, Arrangement, and Management of Fresh-water and Marine Aquaria; containing Full Information as to the Plants, Weeds, Fish, Molluscs, Insects. &c., How and Where to Obtain Them, and How to Keep Them in Health. Illustrated. By REV. GREGORY C. BATEMAN, A.K.C., and REGINALD A. R. BENNETT, B.A. *In cloth gilt, price 5s. 6d., by post 5s. 10d.*

AQUARIA, FRESHWATER: Their Construction, Arrangement, Stocking, and Management. Fully Illustrated. By REV. G. C. BATEMAN, A.K.C. *In cloth gilt, price 3s. 6d., by post 3s. 10d.*

AQUARIA, MARINE: Their Construction, Arrangement, and Management. Fully Illustrated. By R. A. R. BENNETT, B.A. *In cloth gilt, price 2s. 6d., by post 2s. 9d.*

AUSTRALIA, SHALL I TRY? A Guide to the Australian Colonies for the Emigrant Settler and Business Man. With two Illustrations. By GEORGE LACON JAMES. *In cloth gilt, price 3s. 6d., by post 3s. 10d.*

AUTOGRAPH COLLECTING: A Practical Manual for Amateurs and Historical Students, containing ample information on the Selection and Arrangement of Autographs, the Detection of Forged Specimens. &c., &c., to which are added numerous Facsimiles for Study and Reference, and an extensive Valuation Table of Autographs worth Collecting. By HENRY T. SCOTT, M.D., L.R.C.P., &c., Rector of Swettenham, Cheshire. *In leatherette gilt, price 7s. 6d., by post 7s. 10d.*

BEES AND BEE-KEEPING: Scientific and Practical. By F. R. CHESHIRE, F.L.S., F.R.M.S., Lecturer on Apiculture at South Kensington. *In two vols., cloth gilt, price 16s., by post 16s. 4d.*

Vol. I., Scientific. A complete Treatise on the Anatomy and Physiology of the Hive Bee. *In cloth gilt, price 7s. 6d., by post 7s. 10d.*

Vol. II., Practical Management of Bees. An Exhaustive Treatise on Advanced Bee Culture. *In cloth gilt, price 8s. 6d., by post 8s. 10d*

BEE-KEEPING, BOOK OF. A very practical and Complete Manual on the Proper Management of Bees, especially written for Beginners and Amateurs who have but a few Hives Fully Illustrated. By W. B. Webster, First-class Expert, B B K A *In paper, price 1s., by post 1s. 2d ; cloth, 1s. 6d., by post 1s. 8d.*

BEGONIA CULTURE, for Amateurs and Professionals. Containing Full Directions for the Successful Cultivation of the Begonia, under Glass and in the Open Air Illustrated. By B C Ravenscroft. *In paper, price 1s., by post 1s. 2d.*

BENT IRON WORK: A Practical Manual of Instruction for Amateurs in the Art and Craft of Making and Ornamenting Light Articles in imitation of the beautiful Mediæval and Italian Wrought Iron Work. By F. J. Erskine. Illustrated. *In paper, price 1s , by post 1s 2d.*

BOAT BUILDING AND SAILING, PRACTICAL. Containing Full Instructions for Designing and Building Punts, Skiffs, Canoes, Sailing Boats, &c. Particulars of the most suitable Sailing Boats and Yachts for Amateurs, and Instructions for their Proper Handling. Fully Illustrated with Designs and Working Diagrams. By Adrian Neison, C.E , Dixon Kemp, A.I.N A., and G. Christopher Davies *In one vol., cloth gilt, price 7s. 6d., by post 7s. 10d.*

BOAT BUILDING FOR AMATEURS, PRACTICAL. Containing Full Instructions for Designing and Building Punts, Skiffs, Canoes, Sailing Boats, &c. Fully Illustrated with Working Diagrams. By Adrian Neison, C E. Second Edition, Revised and Enlarged by Dixon Kemp, Author of "Yacht Designing," "A Manual of Yacht and Boat Sailing," &c *In cloth gilt, price 2s. 6d., by post 2s 9d*

BOAT SAILING FOR AMATEURS. Containing Particulars of the most Suitable Sailing Boats and Yachts for Amateurs, and Instructions for their Proper Handling, &c. Illustrated with numerous Diagrams By G. Christopher Davies Second Edition, Revised and Enlarged, and with several New Plans of Yachts. *In cloth gilt, price 5s., by post 5s. 4d.*

BOOKBINDING FOR AMATEURS: Being Descriptions of the various Tools and Appliances Required, and Minute Instructions for their Effective Use By W. J. E. Crane Illustrated with 156 Engravings *In cloth gilt, price 2s. 6d., by post 2s 9d*

BUNKUM ENTERTAINMENTS: A Collection of Original Laughable Skits on Conjuring, Physiognomy, Juggling, Performing Fleas, Waxworks, Panorama, Phrenology, Phonograph, Second Sight, Lightning Calculators, Ventriloquism, Spiritualism, &c, to which are added Humorous Sketches, Whimsical Recitals, and Drawing-room Comedies. *In cloth, price 2s. 6d , by post 2s. 9d.*

BUTTERFLIES, THE BOOK OF BRITISH: A Practical Manual for Collectors and Naturalists Splendidly Illustrated throughout with very accurate Engravings of the Caterpillars, Chrysalids, and Butterflies, both upper and under sides, from drawings by the Author or direct from Nature. By W. J. Lucas, B.A. *Price 3s. 6d , by post 3s 9d*

BUTTERFLY AND MOTH COLLECTING: Where to Search, and What to Do. By G. E. SIMMS. Illustrated. *In paper, price* 1s., *by post* 1s. 2d.

CACTUS CULTURE FOR AMATEURS: Being Descriptions of the various Cactuses grown in this country; with Full and Practical Instructions for their Successful Cultivation. By W. WATSON, Assistant Curator of the Royal Botanic Gardens, Kew. Profusely Illustrated. *In cloth gilt, price* 5s., *by post* 5s. 3d.

CAGE BIRDS, DISEASES OF: Their Causes, Symptoms, and Treatment. A Handbook for everyone who keeps a Bird. By DR. W. T. GREENE, F.Z.S. *In paper, price* 1s., *by post* 1s. 2d.

CAGE BIRDS, BRITISH. Containing Full Directions for Successfully Breeding, Rearing, and Managing the various British Birds that can be kept in Confinement. Illustrated with COLOURED PLATES and numerous finely-cut Wood Engravings. By R. L. WALLACE. *In cloth gilt, price* 10s. 6d., *by post* 10s. 10d.

CANARY BOOK. Full Directions for the Breeding, Rearing, and Management of all Varieties of Canaries and Canary Mules, and all other matters connected with this Fancy. By ROBERT L. WALLACE. Third Edition. *In cloth gilt, price* 5s., *by post* 5s. 4d.; *with COLOURED PLATES*, 6s. 6d., *by post* 6s. 10d.; and in Sections as follows:

    General Management of Canaries. Cages and Cage-making, Breeding, Managing, Mule Breeding, Diseases and their Treatment, Moulting, Pests, &c. Illustrated. *In cloth, price* 2s. 6d., *by post* 2s. 9d.

    Exhibition Canaries. Full Particulars of all the different Varieties, their Points of Excellence, Preparing Birds for Exhibition, Formation and Management of Canary Societies and Exhibitions. Illustrated. *In cloth, price* 2s. 6d., *by post* 2s. 9d.

CANOE BUILDING FOR AMATEURS: A Practical Manual, with Plans, Working Diagrams, and full Instructions. By COTTERILL SCHOLEFIELD. *Price* 2s. 6d., *by post* 2s. 9d.   [*In the Press.*

CARD TRICKS, BOOK OF, for Drawing-room and Stage Entertainments by Amateurs; with an exposure of Tricks as practised by Card Sharpers and Swindlers. Numerous Illustrations. By PROF. R. KUNARD. *In illustrated wrapper, price* 2s. 6d., *by post* 2s. 9d.

CATS, DOMESTIC OR FANCY: A Practical Treatise on their Antiquity, Domestication, Varieties, Breeding, Management, Diseases and Remedies, Exhibition and Judging. By JOHN JENNINGS. Illustrated. *In cloth, price* 2s. 6d., *by post* 2s. 9d.

CHRYSANTHEMUM CULTURE, for Amateurs and Professionals. Containing Full Directions for the Successful Cultivation of the Chrysanthemum for Exhibition and the Market. Illustrated. By B. C. RAVENSCROFT. *In paper, price* 1s., *by post* 1s. 2d.

COINS, A GUIDE TO ENGLISH PATTERN, in Gold, Silver, Copper, and Pewter, from Edward I. to Victoria, with their Value. By the REV. G. F. CROWTHER, M.A. Illustrated. *In silver cloth, with gilt facsimiles of Coins, price* 5s., *by post* 5s. 3d.

COINS OF GREAT BRITAIN AND IRELAND, A GUIDE TO THE, in Gold, Silver and Copper, from the Earliest Period to the Present Time, with their Value. By the late Colonel W. STEWART

THORBURN With 27 Plates in Gold, Silver, and Copper, and 8 Plates of Gold and Silver Coins in RAISED FACSIMILE. *In cloth, with silver facsimiles of Coins, price 7s 6d , by post 7s. 10d.*

COLLIE, THE. Its History, Points, and Breeding. By HUGH DALZIEL. Illustrated with Coloured Frontispiece and Plates. *In paper, price 1s., by post 1s. 2d ; cloth, 2s , by post 2s. 3d*

COLLIE STUD BOOK. Edited by HUGH DALZIEL *Price 3s. 6d. each, by post 3s. 9d. each.*

Vol. I., containing Pedigrees of 1308 of the best-known Dogs, traced to their most remote known ancestors ; Show Record to Feb., 1890, &c.

Vol. II. Pedigrees of 795 Dogs, Show Record, &c.

Vol. III. Pedigrees of 786 Dogs, Show Record, &c.

COLUMBARIUM, MOORE'S. Reprinted Verbatim from the original Edition of 1735, with a Brief Notice of the Author. By W B. TEGETMEIER, F Z S , Member of the British Ornithologists' Union. *Price 1s., by post 1s. 2d*

CONJURING, BOOK OF MODERN. A Practical Guide to Drawing-room and Stage Magic for Amateurs. By PROFESSOR R. KUNARD. Illustrated. *In illustrated wrapper, price 2s. 6d., by post 2s. 9d.*

COOKERY FOR AMATEURS ; or, French Dishes for English Homes of all Classes. Includes Simple Cookery, Middle-class Cookery, Superior Cookery, Cookery for Invalids, and Breakfast and Luncheon Cookery. By MADAME VALÉRIE. Second Edition. *In paper, price 1s., by post 1s 2d.*

CUCUMBER CULTURE FOR AMATEURS. Including also Melons, Vegetable Marrows, and Gourds. Illustrated. By W. J MAY. *In paper, price 1s., by post 1s 2d*

CYCLES OF 1893, with Special Chapters on Tyres and Accessories. By CHARLES W. HARTUNG (Stanley Cycling Club). Illustrated *In paper, price 1s , by post 1s. 2d.*

CYCLIST'S ROUTE MAP of England and Wales. The Third Edition, thoroughly Revised Shows clearly all the Main, and most of the Cross, Roads, and the Distances between the Chief Towns, as well as the Mileage from London. In addition to this, Routes of *Thirty of the most Interesting Tours* are printed in red. The map is mounted on linen, and is the fullest, handiest, and best tourist's map in the market *In cloth, price 1s , by post 1s. 2d*

DOGS, BREAKING AND TRAINING : Being Concise Directions for the proper education of Dogs, both for the Field and for Companions. Second Edition. By "PATHFINDER." With Chapters by HUGH DALZIEL. Illustrated *In cloth gilt, price 6s. 6d., by post 6s. 10d*

DOGS, BRITISH, ANCIENT AND MODERN : Their Varieties, History, and Characteristics By HUGH DALZIEL, assisted by Eminent Fanciers. SECOND EDITION, Revised and Enlarged. Illustrated with First-class COLOURED PLATES and full-page Engravings of Dogs of the Day. This is the fullest work on the various breeds of dogs kept in England. In three volumes, *demy 8vo, cloth gilt, price 10s. 6d. each, by post 11s. 1d. each.*

Dogs Used in Field Sports. Containing Particulars of the following among other Breeds : Greyhound, Irish Wolfhound, Bloodhound, Foxhound, Harrier, Basset, Dachshund, Pointer, Setters, Spaniels, and Retrievers. SEVEN COLOURED PLATES and 21 full-page Engravings.

Dogs Useful to Man in other Work than Field Sports; **House and Toy Dogs.** Containing Particulars of the following, among other Breeds: Collie, Bulldog, Mastiff, St. Bernards, Newfoundland, Great Dane, Fox and all other Terriers, King Charles and Blenheim Spaniels, Pug, Pomeranian, Poodle, Italian Greyhound, Toy Dogs, &c., &c. COLOURED PLATES and full-page Engravings.

Practical Kennel Management: A Complete Treatise on all Matters relating to the Proper Management of Dogs, whether kept for the Show Bench, for the Field, or for Companions. Illustrated with Coloured and numerous other Plates. [*In the Press.*

DOGS, DISEASES OF: Their Causes, Symptoms, and Treatment; Modes of Administering Medicines, Treatment in cases of Poisoning, &c. For the use of Amateurs. By HUGH DALZIEL. Third Edition. *In paper, price 1s., by post 1s. 2d.; in cloth gilt, 2s., by post 2s. 3d*

ENTERTAINMENTS, AMATEUR, FOR CHARITABLE AND OTHER OBJECTS: How to Organize and Work them with Profit and Success. By ROBERT GANTHONY. *In coloured cover, price 1s., by post 1s. 2d.*

FANCY WORK SERIES, ARTISTIC. A Series of Illustrated Manuals on Artistic and Popular Fancy Work of various kinds. Each number is complete in itself, and issued at the uniform *price of 6d., by post 7d.* Now ready—(1) MACRAMÉ LACE (Second Edition); (2) PATCHWORK, (3) TATTING; (4) CREWEL WORK, (5) APPLIQUÉ, (6) FANCY NETTING.

FERNS, THE BOOK OF CHOICE: for the Garden, Conservatory, and Stove. Describing the best and most striking Ferns and Selaginellas, and giving explicit directions for their Cultivation, the formation of Rockeries, the arrangement of Ferneries, &c. By GEORGE SCHNEIDER. With numerous Coloured Plates and other Illustrations. *In 3 vols., large post 4to. Cloth gilt, price £3 3s., by post £3 6s.*

FERNS, CHOICE BRITISH. Descriptive of the most beautiful Variations from the common forms, and their Culture. By C. T. DRUERY, F.L.S. Very accurate PLATES, and other Illustrations. *In cloth gilt, price 2s. 6d., by post 2s. 9d.*

FERRETS AND FERRETING. Containing Instructions for the Breeding, Management, and Working of Ferrets Second Edition, Rewritten and greatly Enlarged. Illustrated. *In paper, price 6d., by post 7d.*

FERTILITY OF EGGS CERTIFICATE. These are Forms of Guarantee given by the Sellers to the Buyers of Eggs for Hatching, undertaking to refund value of any unfertile eggs, or to replace them with good ones Very valuable to sellers of eggs, as they induce purchases. *In books, with counterfoils, price 6d, by post 7d.*

FIREWORK-MAKING FOR AMATEURS. A complete, accurate, and easily-understood work on Making Simple and High-class Fireworks. By Dr. W. H. BROWNE, M.A. *In paper, price 2s. 6d., by post 2s 9d.*

FOREIGN BIRDS, FAVOURITE, for Cages and Aviaries How to Keep them in Health Fully Illustrated. By W. T. GREENE, M.A., M.D., F.Z.S., &c. *In cloth, price 2s. 6d, by post 2s. 9d.*

FOX TERRIER, THE. Its History, Points, Breeding, Rearing, Preparing, for Exhibition, and Coursing. By HUGH DALZIEL. Illustrated with Coloured Frontispiece and Plates. *In paper, price 1s, by post 1s. 2d., cloth, 2s., by post 2s. 3d.*

FOX TERRIER STUD BOOK. Edited by HUGH DALZIEL. *Price 3s 6d. each., by post 3s 9d each.*

Vol. I., containing Pedigrees of over 1400 of the best-known Dogs, traced to their most remote known ancestors.

Vol. II. Pedigrees of 1544 Dogs, Show Record, &c.

Vol. III. Pedigrees of 1214 Dogs, Show Record, &c.

Vol. IV. Pedigrees of 1168 Dogs, Show Record, &c.

Vol. V. Pedigrees of 1662 Dogs, Show Record, &c.

FRETWORK AND MARQUETERIE. A Practical Manual of Instructions in the Art of Fret-cutting and Marqueterie Work. By D. DENNING. *In paper, price 1s., by post 1s. 2d.* [*In the Press*

FRIESLAND MERES, A CRUISE ON THE. By ERNEST R. SUFFLING Illustrated from Photos and Special Drawings. *In paper, price 1s., by post 1s 2d.*

GAME AND GAME SHOOTING, NOTES ON. Miscellaneous Observations on Birds and Animals, and on the Sport they afford for the Gun in Great Britain, including Grouse, Partridges, Pheasants, Hares, Rabbits, Quails, Woodcocks, Snipe, and Rooks. By J. J. MANLEY, M.A. Illustrated. *In cloth gilt, price 7s. 6d., by post 7s 10d.*

GAME PRESERVING, PRACTICAL. Containing the fullest Directions for Rearing and Preserving both Winged and Ground Game, and Destroying Vermin; with other Information of Value to the Game Preserver. Illustrated. By WILLIAM CARNEGIE. *In cloth gilt, demy 8vo, price 21s., by post 21s. 9d.*

GARDENING, DICTIONARY OF. A Practical Encyclopædia of Horticulture, for Amateurs and Professionals. Illustrated with 2440 Engravings. Edited by G. NICHOLSON, Curator of the Royal Botanic Gardens, Kew; assisted by Prof. Trail, M.D., Rev. P. W. Myles, B A., F.L S , W. Watson, J. Garrett, and other Specialists. *In 4 vols , large post 4to. In cloth gilt, price £3, by post £3 3s.*

GOAT, BOOK OF THE. Containing Full Particulars of the various Breeds of Goats, and their Profitable Management. With many Plates. By H STEPHEN HOLMES PEGLER Third Edition, with Engravings and Coloured Frontispiece. *In cloth gilt, price 4s 6d , by post 4s. 10d.*

GOAT-KEEPING FOR AMATEURS: Being the Practical Management of Goats for Milking Purposes. Abridged from "The Book of the Goat." Illustrated. *In paper, price 1s., by post 1s. 2d.*

GRAPE GROWING FOR AMATEURS. A Thoroughly Practical Book on Successful Vine Culture. By E. MOLYNEUX. Illustrated. *In paper, price 1s , by post 1s. 2d.*

GREENHOUSE MANAGEMENT FOR AMATEURS. Descriptions of the Best Greenhouses and Frames, with Instructions for Building them, particulars of the various methods of Heating, Illustrated Descriptions of the most suitable Plants, with general and Special Cultural Directions, and all necessary information for the Guidance of the Amateur. Second Edition, Revised and Enlarged. Magnificently Illustrated. By W. J. MAY. *In cloth gilt, price 5s , by post 5s. 4d.*

GREYHOUND, THE: Its History, Points, Breeding, Rearing, Training, and Running. By HUGH DALZIEL. With Coloured Frontispiece *In cloth gilt, demy 8vo, price 2s. 6d., by post 2s 9d.*

GUINEA PIG, THE, for Food, Fur, and Fancy. Illustrated with Coloured Frontispiece and Engravings. An exhaustive book on the Varieties of the Guinea Pig, and its Management. By C. CUMBERLAND, F.Z.S. *In cloth gilt, price 2s. 6d., by post 2s. 9d.*

HAND CAMERA MANUAL, THE. A Practical Handbook on all Matters connected with the Use of the Hand Camera in Photography. Illustrated. By W. D. WELFORD. *Price 1s., by post 1s. 2d.*

HANDWRITING, CHARACTER INDICATED BY. With Illustrations in Support of the Theories advanced taken from Autograph Letters of Statesmen, Lawyers, Soldiers, Ecclesiastics, Authors, Poets, Musicians, Actors, and other persons. Second Edition. By R. BAUGHAN. *In cloth gilt, price 2s. 6d., by post 2s. 9d.*

HARDY PERENNIALS and Old-fashioned Garden Flowers. Descriptions, alphabetically arranged, of the most desirable Plants for Borders, Rockeries, and Shrubberies, including Foliage as well as Flowering Plants. Profusely Illustrated. By J. WOOD. *In cloth, price 5s., by post 5s. 4d.*

HOME MEDICINE AND SURGERY: A Dictionary of Diseases and Accidents, and their proper Home Treatment. For Family Use. By W. J. MACKENZIE, M.D., Medical Officer for Lower Holloway, Medical Referee for North London of the Scottish Provincial Assurance Company, late Lecturer to the St. John's Ambulance Association, Author of the "Medical Management of Children," &c. Illustrated. *In cloth, price 2s. 6d., by post 2s. 9d.*

HORSE-KEEPER, THE PRACTICAL. By GEORGE FLEMING, C.B., LL.D., F.R.C.V.S., late Principal Veterinary Surgeon to the British Army, and Ex-President of the Royal College of Veterinary Surgeons. *In cloth, price 3s. 6d., by post 3s. 10d.*

HORSE-KEEPING FOR AMATEURS. A Practical Manual on the Management of Horses, for the guidance of those who keep one or two for their personal use. By FOX RUSSELL. *In paper, price 1s., by post 1s. 2d.; cloth, 2s., by post 2s. 3d.*

HORSES, DISEASES OF: Their Causes, Symptoms, and Treatment. For the use of Amateurs. By HUGH DALZIEL. *In paper, price 1s., by post 1s. 2d.; cloth 2s., by post 2s. 3d.*

INLAND WATERING PLACES. A Description of the Spas of Great Britain and Ireland, their Mineral Waters, and their Medicinal Value, and the attractions which they offer to Invalids and other Visitors. Profusely illustrated. A Companion Volume to "Seaside Watering Places.' *In cloth, price 2s. 6d., by post 2s. 10d.*

JOURNALISM, PRACTICAL: How to Enter Thereon and Succeed. A book for all who think of "writing for the Press." By JOHN DAWSON. *In cloth gilt, price 2s. 6d., by post 2s. 9d.*

LAYING HENS, HOW TO KEEP and to Rear Chickens in Large or Small Numbers, in Absolute Confinement, with Perfect Success. By MAJOR G. F. MORANT. *In paper, price 6d., by post 7d.*

LEGAL PROFESSION, A GUIDE TO THE. A Practical Treatise on the various Methods of Entering either Branch of the Legal Profession; also a Course of Study for each of the Examinations, and selected Papers of Questions; forming a Complete Guide to every Department of Legal Preparation. By J. H. SLATER, Barrister-at-Law, of the Middle Temple. *In cloth, price 7s. 6d., by post 7s. 10d.*

LIBRARY MANUAL, THE. A Guide to the Formation of a Library, and the Values of Rare and Standard Books. By J. H. SLATER, Barrister-at-Law. Third Edition. Revised and Greatly Enlarged. *In cloth gilt, price 7s. 6d., by post 7s. 10d.*

MICE, FANCY: Their Varieties, Management, and Breeding. Re-issue, with Criticisms and Notes by DR. CARTER BLAKE. Illustrated. *In paper, price 6d., by post 7d.*

MODEL YACHTS AND BOATS: Their Designing, Making, and Sailing. Illustrated with 118 Designs and Working Diagrams. A splendid book for boys and others interested in making and rigging toy boats for sailing. It is the best book on the subject now published. By J DU V GROSVENOR. *In leatherette, price 5s, by post 5s. 3d.*

MONKEYS, PET, and How to Manage Them Illustrated. By ARTHUR PATTERSON. *In cloth gilt, price 2s. 6d., by post 2s. 9d.*

MUSHROOM CULTURE FOR AMATEURS. With Full Directions for Successful Growth in Houses, Sheds Cellars, and Pots, on Shelves, and Out of Doors. Illustrated. By W. J. MAY. *In paper, price 1s, by post 1s. 2d.*

NATURAL HISTORY SKETCHES among the Carnivora—Wild and Domesticated; with Observations on their Habits and Mental Faculties. By ARTHUR NICOLS, F.G.S., F.R.G S Illustrated *In cloth gilt, price 5s, by post 5s. 4d.*

NEEDLEWORK, DICTIONARY OF. An Encyclopædia of Artistic, Plain, and Fancy Needlework; Plain, practical, complete, and magnificently Illustrated. By S. F. A. CAULFEILD and B. C. SAWARD. Accepted by H.M. the Queen, H.R H. the Princess of Wales, H.R H. the Duchess of Edinburgh, H.R.H. the Duchess of Connaught, and H.R.H. the Duchess of Albany. Dedicated by special permission to H.R.H. Princess Louise, Marchioness of Lorne. *In demy 4to, 528pp., 829 Illustrations, extra cloth gilt, plain edges, cushioned bevelled boards, price 21s., by post 22s.; with COLOURED PLATES, elegant satin brocade cloth binding, and coloured edges, 31s. 6d., by post 32s 6d*

ORCHIDS: Their Culture and Management, with Descriptions of all the Kinds in General Cultivation Illustrated by Coloured Plates and Engravings. By W. WATSON, Assistant-Curator, Royal Botanic Gardens, Kew, Assisted by W. BEAN, Foreman, Royal Gardens, Kew. Second Edition, Revised and with Extra Plates *In cloth gilt and gilt edges, price £1 1s., by post £1 2s.*

PAINTING, DECORATIVE. A practical Handbook on Painting and Etching upon Textiles, Pottery, Porcelain, Paper, Vellum, Leather, Glass, Wood, Stone, Metals, and Plaster, for the Decoration of our Homes. By B. C. SAWARD. *In cloth, price 5s., by post 5s. 4d.*

PARCEL POST DISPATCH BOOK (registered) An invaluable book for all who send parcels by post. Provides Address Labels, Certificate of Posting, and Record of Parcels Dispatched By the use of this book parcels are insured against loss or damage to the extent of £2. Authorized by the Post Office. *Price 1s., by post 1s 2d., for 100 parcels; larger sizes if required.*

PARROT, THE GREY, and How to Treat it. By W. T GREENE, M D , M A , F Z S , &c *Price 1s , by post 1s. 2d.*

PARROTS, THE SPEAKING. The Art of Keeping and Breeding the principal Talking Parrots in Confinement. By DR. KARL RUSS. Illustrated with COLOURED PLATES and Engravings. *In cloth gilt, price 5s., by post 5s. 4d.*

PATIENCE, GAMES OF, for one or more Players. A very clearly-written and well-illustrated Book of Instructions on How to play 106 different Games of Patience. By MISS WHITMORE JONES. Illustrated. Series I, thirty-nine games, 1s, by post 1s 2d ; Series II., thirty-four games, 1s., by post 1s 2d ; Series III, thirty-three games, 1s by post 1s 2d. *The three bound together in cloth, price 3s 6d., by post 3s. 10d.* (A copy has been graciously accepted by H M. the Queen)

PEN PICTURES AND HOW TO DRAW THEM. A Practical Handbook on the various Methods of Illustrating in Black and White for "Process" Engraving, with numerous Designs, Diagrams, and Sketches. By ERIC MEADE. *In cloth gilt, price 2s. 6d., by post 2s. 9d.*

PERSPECTIVE, THE ESSENTIALS OF. With numerous Illustrations drawn by the Author. By L. W. MILLER, Principal of the School of Industrial Art of the Pennsylvania Museum, Philadelphia. This book is such a manual as has long been desired for the guidance of art students and for self-instruction. The instructions are clearly set forth, and the principles are vividly enforced by a large number of attractive drawings. *Price 6s. 6d., by post 6s. 10d.*

PHEASANT-KEEPING FOR AMATEURS. A Practical Handbook on the Breeding, Rearing, and General Management of Fancy Pheasants in Confinement. By GEO. HORNE. Illustrated with Diagrams of the necessary Pens, Aviaries, &c., and a COLOURED FRONTISPIECE and many full-page Engravings of the chief Varieties of Pheasants, drawn from life by A. F. LYDON. *In cloth gilt, price 3s. 6d., by post 3s. 9d.*

PHOTOGRAPHY (MODERN) FOR AMATEURS. By J. EATON FEARN. *In paper, price 1s., by post 1s. 2d.*

PICTURE-FRAME MAKING FOR AMATEURS. Being Practical Instructions in the Making of various kinds of Frames for Paintings, Drawings, Photographs, and Engravings. Illustrated. By the REV. J. LUKIN. *Cheap Edition, in paper, price 1s., by post 1s. 2d.*

PIG, BOOK OF THE. The Selection, Breeding, Feeding, and Management of the Pig; the Treatment of its Diseases; the Curing and Preserving of Hams, Bacon, and other Pork Foods; and other information appertaining to Pork Farming. By PROFESSOR JAMES LONG. Fully Illustrated with Portraits of Prize Pigs, Plans of Model Piggeries, &c. *In cloth gilt, price 10s. 6d., by post 11s. 1d.*

PIG-KEEPING, PRACTICAL: A Manual for Amateurs, based on Personal Experience in Breeding, Feeding, and Fattening; also in Buying and Selling Pigs at Market Prices. By R. D. GARRATT. *In paper, price 1s., by post 1s. 2d.*

PIGEONS, FANCY. Containing Full Directions for the Breeding and Management of Fancy Pigeons, and Descriptions of every known Variety, together with all other information of interest or use to Pigeon Fanciers. Third Edition, bringing the subject down to the present time. 18 COLOURED PLATES, and 22 other full-page Illustrations. By J. C. LYELL. *In cloth gilt, price 10s. 6d., by post 10s. 10d.*

PIGEON-KEEPING FOR AMATEURS. A complete Guide to the Amateur Breeder of Domestic and Fancy Pigeons. By J. C. LYELL. Illustrated. *In cloth, price 2s. 6d., by post 2s. 9d.*

POKER BOOK, THE. How to Play Poker with Success. By R. GUERNDALE. *In paper, price 1s., by post 1s. 2d.*

POLISHES AND STAINS FOR WOODS: A Complete Guide to Polishing Woodwork, with Directions for Staining, and Full Information for making the Stains, Polishes, &c., in the simplest and most satisfactory manner. By DAVID DENNING. *In paper, price 1s., by post 1s. 2d.*

POOL, GAMES OF. Describing Various English and American Pool Games, and giving the Rules in full. Illustrated. *In paper, price 1s., by post 1s. 2d.*

POULTRY-KEEPING, POPULAR.   A Practical and Complete Guide to Breeding and Keeping Poultry for Eggs or for the Table.   By F. A. Mackenzie.   Illustrated.   *In paper, price* 1s., *by post* 1s. 2d.

POULTRY AND PIGEON DISEASES: Their Causes, Symptoms, and Treatment.   A Practical Manual for all Fanciers.   By Quintin Craig and James Lyell.   *In paper, price* 1s., *by post* 1s. 2d.

POULTRY FOR PRIZES AND PROFIT.   Contains: Breeding Poultry for Prizes, Exhibition Poultry and Management of the Poultry Yard.   Handsomely Illustrated.   Second Edition.   By Prof. James Long.   *In cloth gilt, price* 2s. 6d., *by post* 2s. 9d.

PYROGRAPHY OR POKER WORK.   By Mrs. Maud Maude.   With Fifty-two Original Illustrations and Designs by Wm. Freeman.   *In paper, price* 1s. 6d., *by post* 1s. 8d.; *cloth,* 2s. 6d., *by post* 2s. 9d.

RABBIT, BOOK OF THE.   A Complete Work on Breeding and Rearing all Varieties of Fancy Rabbits, giving their History, Variations, Uses, Points, Selection, Mating, Management, &c., &c.   SECOND EDITION.   Edited by Kempster W. Knight.   Illustrated with Coloured and other Plates.   *In cloth gilt, price* 10s. 6d., *by post* 11s.

RABBITS, DISEASES OF: Their Causes, Symptoms, and Cure.   With a Chapter on The Diseases of Cavies.   Reprinted from "The Book of the Rabbit" and "The Guinea Pig for Food, Fur, and Fancy."   *In paper, price* 1s., *by post* 1s. 2d.

RABBIT-FARMING, PROFITABLE.   A Practical Manual, showing how Hutch Rabbit-farming in the Open can be made to Pay Well.   By Major G. F. Morant.   *In paper, price* 1s., *by post* 1s. 2d.

RABBITS FOR PRIZES AND PROFIT.   Containing Full Directions for the Proper Management of Fancy Rabbits in Health and Disease, for Pets or the Market, and Descriptions of every known Variety, with Instructions for Breeding Good Specimens.   Illustrated.   By Charles Rayson.   *In cloth gilt, price* 2s. 6d., *by post* 2s. 9d.
Also in Sections, as follows:—

General Management of Rabbits.   Including Hutches, Breeding, Feeding, Diseases and their Treatment, Rabbit Courts, &c.   Fully Illustrated.   *In paper, price* 1s., *by post* 1s. 2d.

Exhibition Rabbits.   Being descriptions of all Varieties of Fancy Rabbits, their Points of Excellence, and how to obtain them.   Illustrated.   *In paper, price* 1s., *by post* 1s. 2d.

REPOUSSÉ WORK FOR AMATEURS: Being the Art of Ornamenting Thin Metal with Raised Figures.   By L. L. Haslope.   Illustrated.   *In cloth gilt, price* 2s. 6d., *by post* 2s. 9d.

ROSES FOR AMATEURS.   A Practical Guide to the Selection and Cultivation of the best Roses, either for Exhibition or mere Pleasure, by that large section of the Gardening World, the Amateur Lover of Roses.   Illustrated.   By the Rev. J. Honywood D'Ombrain, Hon. Sec. of the National Rose Society.   *In paper, price* 1s., *by post* 1s. 2d.

SAILING GUIDE TO THE SOLENT AND POOLE HARBOUR, with Practical Hints as to Living and Cooking on, and Working a Small Yacht.   By Lieut.-Colonel T. G. Cuthell.   Illustrated with Coloured Charts.   *In cloth, price* 2s. 6d., *by post* 2s. 9d.

SAILING TOURS.   The Yachtman's Guide to the Cruising Waters of the English and Adjacent Coasts.   By Frank Cowper, B.A.

Vol. I., the Coasts of Essex and Suffolk, containing Descriptions of every Creek from the Thames to Aldborough. Numerous Charts and Illustrations. *In cloth, price 5s., by post 5s. 3d.*

Vol. II. The South Coast, from the Thames to the Scilly Islands, with twenty-five Charts printed in Colours. *In cloth, price 7s. 6d., by post 7s. 10d.*

Vol. III. The Coast of Brittany, including the Departments of Finisterre the Morbihan, and the Lower Loire. Containing Descriptions of every Creek, Harbour, and Roadstead from L'Abervrach to St. Nazaire, with an Account of the Loire and its celebrated Castles. With twelve Charts, printed in Colours *In crown 8vo, cloth gilt, price 7s. 6d, by post 7s. 10d. With larger Charts, mounted on linen 10s 6d., by post 11s. Charts separately 3s., by post 3s. 3d.*

ST. BERNARD, THE. Its History, Points, Breeding, and Rearing. By HUGH DALZIEL. Illustrated with Coloured Frontispiece and Plates. *In cloth, price 2s. 6d., by post 2s 9d.*

ST. BERNARD STUD BOOK. Edited by HUGH DALZIEL. *Price 3s. 6d each, by post 3s. 9d. each.*

Vol. I. Pedigrees of 1278 of the best known Dogs, traced to their most remote known ancestors, Show Record, &c.

Vol. II. Pedigrees of 564 Dogs, Show Record, &c.

SEA-FISHING FOR AMATEURS. Practical Instructions to Visitors at Seaside Places for Catching Sea-Fish from Pier-heads, Shore, or Boats, principally by means of Hand Lines, with a very useful List of Fishing Stations, the Fish to be caught there, and the Best Seasons. By FRANK HUDSON. Illustrated. *In paper, price 1s., by post 1s 2d.*

SEA-FISHING ON THE ENGLISH COAST. A Manual of Practical Instruction on the Art of Making and Using Sea-Tackle. With a full account of the methods in vogue during each month of the year, and a Detailed Guide for Sea-Fishermen to all the most Popular Watering Places on the English Coast. By FREDERICK G. AFLALO. Illustrated. *In cloth, price 2s. 6d., by post 2s. 9d.*

SEASIDE WATERING PLACES. A Description of nearly 200 Holiday Resorts on the Coasts of England and Wales, the Channel Islands, and the Isle of Man, including the gayest and most quiet places, giving full particulars of them and their attractions, and all other information likely to assist persons in selecting places in which to spend their Holidays according to their individual tastes; with BUSINESS DIRECTORY of Tradesmen, arranged in order of the Towns. Illustrated. *In cloth, price 2s 6d, by post 2s. 10d.* [*7th Edition in the Press.*

SHAVE, AN EASY: The Mysteries, Secrets, and Whole Art of, laid bare for 1s., by post 1s. 2d. Edited by JOSEPH MORTON.

SHEET METAL, WORKING IN: Being Practical Instructions for Making and Mending Small Articles in Tin, Copper, Iron, Zinc, and Brass. Illustrated. Third Edition By the Rev. J. LUKIN, B.A. *In paper, price 1s., by post 1s. 1d.*

SHORTHAND, ON GURNEY'S SYSTEM (IMPROVED), LESSONS IN. Being Instructions in the Art of Shorthand Writing as used in the Service of the two Houses of Parliament. By R. E. MILLER. *In paper, price 1s., by post 1s. 2d.*

SHORTHAND, EXERCISES IN, for Daily Half Hours, on a Newly-devised and Simple Method, free from the Labour of Learning. Illustrated step by step. Being Part II. of " Lessons in Shorthand on Gurney's System (Improved)." By R. E. MILLER. *In paper, price 9d., by post 10d.*

SHORTHAND SYSTEMS; WHICH IS THE BEST? Being a Discussion, by various Experts, on the Merits and Demerits of all the principal Systems, with Illustrative Examples   Edited by THOMAS ANDERSON. *In paper, price 1s, by post 1s. 2d*

SICK NURSING AT HOME: Being Plain Directions and Hints for the Proper Nursing of Sick Persons, and the Home Treatment of Diseases and Accidents in cases of Sudden Emergencies. By S F. A. CAULFEILD. *In paper, price 1s, by post 1s. 2d.; cloth, 1s 6d., by post 1s. 8d.*

SKATING CARDS: An Easy Method of Learning Figure Skating, as the Cards *can be used on the Ice. In cloth case, 2s. 6d. by post 2s 9d : leather, 3s. 6d., by post 3s 9d* A cheap form is issued printed on paper and made up as a small book, 1s., *by post 1s. 1d.*

SLEIGHT OF HAND. A Practical Manual of Legerdemain for Amateurs and Others.   New Edition, Revised and Enlarged.   Profusely Illustrated.   By E. SACHS.   *In cloth gilt, price 6s. 6d., by post 6s. 10d.*

SNAKES, MARSUPIALS, AND BIRDS. A Charming Book of Anecdotes, Adventures, and Zoological Notes relating to Snakes, Marsupials, and Birds.   A capital Book for Boys, and all interested in Popular Natural History.   By ARTHUR NICOLS, F.G S., F R G.S., &c.   Illustrated.   *In cloth gilt, price 5s, by post 5s. 4d.*

TAXIDERMY, PRACTICAL. A Manual of Instruction to the Amateur in Collecting, Preserving, and Setting-up Natural History Specimens of all kinds.   Fully Illustrated with Examples and Working Diagrams   By MONTAGU BROWNE, F.Z.S., Curator of Leicester Museum.   Second Edition   *In cloth gilt, price 7s. 6d, by post 7s. 10d*

THAMES GUIDE BOOK. From Lechlade to Richmond.   For Boating Men, Anglers, Picnic Parties, and all Pleasure-seekers on the River. Arranged on an entirely new plan. Second Edition, profusely illustrated. *In paper, price 1s., by post 1s 3d ; cloth, 1s. 6d, by post 1s 9d.*

TOMATO AND FRUIT GROWING as an Industry for Women. Lectures given at the Forestry Exhibition, Earl's Court, during July and August, 1893   By GRACE HARRIMAN, Practical Fruit Grower and County Council Lecturer.   *In paper, price 1s., by post 1s. 1d*

TOMATO CULTURE FOR AMATEURS. A Practical and very Complete Manual on the Subject.   By B. C. RAVENSCROFT   Illustrated. *In paper, price 1s, by post 1s. 3d.*

TRAPPING, PRACTICAL: Being some Papers on Traps and Trapping for Vermin, with a Chapter on General Bird Trapping and Snaring.   By W. CARNEGIE.   *In paper, price 1s., by post 1s 2d*

TURNING FOR AMATEURS: Being Descriptions of the Lathe and its Attachments and Tools, with Minute Instructions for their Effective Use on Wood, Metal, Ivory, and other Materials.   Second Edition, Revised and Enlarged.   By JAMES LUKIN, B A.   Illustrated with 144 Engravings.   *In cloth gilt, price 2s. 6d., by post 2s 9d.*

TURNING LATHES. A Manual for Technical Schools and Apprentices. A guide to Turning, Screw-cutting, Metal-spinning, &c.   Edited by JAMES LUKIN, B A.   Third Edition.   With 194 Illustrations.   *In cloth gilt, price 3s., by post 3s. 3d.*

VAMPING. A Practical Guide to the Accompaniment of Songs by the Unskilled Musician.   With Examples.   *In paper, price 9d, by post 11d.*

VEGETABLE CULTURE FOR AMATEURS. Containing Concise Directions for the Cultivation of Vegetables in Small Gardens so as to insure Good Crops. . With Lists of the Best Varieties of each Sort. By W. J. MAY. Illustrated. *In paper, price 1s., by post 1s. 2d.*

VENTRILOQUISM, PRACTICAL, AND ITS SISTER ARTS. A thoroughly reliable Guide to the Art of Voice Throwing and Vocal Mimicry ; Vocal Instrumentation ; Ventriloquial Figures ; Entertaining, &c. By ROBERT GANTHONY. Numerous Illustrations. *In cloth, price 2s. 6d., by post 2s. 9d.*

VIOLIN SCHOOL, PRACTICAL, for Home Students. A Practical Book of Instructions and Exercises in Violin Playing, for the use of Amateurs, Self-learners, Teachers, and others. With a supplement on "Easy Legato Studies for the Violin." By J. M. FLEMING. 1 *handsome vol., demy 4to, half Persian, price 9s. 6d., by post 10s. 4d.* Without Supplement, *price 7s. 6d., by post 8s. 1d.*

WAR MEDALS AND DECORATIONS. A Manual for Collectors and for all who are interested in the Achievements of the British Army and Navy, and the Rewards issued in public recognition of them ; with some account of Civil Rewards for Valour. Beautifully Illustrated. By D. HASTINGS IRWIN. *In cloth, price 7s. 6d., by post 7s. 10d.*

WHIPPET AND RACE-DOG, THE : How to Breed, Rear, Train, Race, and Exhibit the Whippet, with the Fullest Particulars relating to the Breed on the Track and Show-Bench, the Management of Race-Meetings, and Original Plans of Courses. By FREEMAN LLOYD, of the National Whippet-Racing Club. *In cloth gilt, price 3s. 6d., by post 3s. 10d.*

WIRE AND SHEET GAUGES OF THE WORLD. Compared and Compiled by C. A. B. PFEILSCHMIDT, of Sheffield. *In paper, price 1s., by post 1s. 1d.*

WOOD CARVING FOR AMATEURS. Containing Descriptions of all the requisite Tools, and Full Instructions for their Use in producing different varieties of Carvings. 2nd Edition, Revised, and with a number of new Illustrations. Edited by D. DENNING. *Price 1s., by post 1s. 2d.*

ROWLANDS' ARTICLES

FOR THE HAIR, COMPLEXION, and TEETH, are the

PUREST AND BEST.

ROWLANDS' ODONTO,

An antiseptic, preservative, and aromatic dentifrice, which whitens the teeth, prevents and arrests decay, and sweetens the breath. It contains no mineral acids, no gritty matter or injurious astringents, keeps the mouth, gums, and teeth free from the unhealthy action of germs in organic matter between the teeth, and is the most wholesome tooth-powder for smokers. **2s. 9d.** per box.

ROWLANDS' MACASSAR OIL

Is the best preserver and beautifier of the hair of children and adults; prevents it falling off or turning grey, eradicates scurf and dandruff, and is also the best brilliantine for ladies' and everybody's use, and as a little goes a very long way it really is most economical for general use; is also sold in a golden colour for fair-haired ladies and children; it contains no lead or mineral ingredients. Bottles, **3s. 6d., 7s., 10s. 6d.**, equal to four small.

ROWLANDS' KALYDOR,

A most cooling, soothing, healing, and refreshing preparation for the Skin and Complexion of Ladies, and all exposed to the summer sun and dust, or the cold and damp of winter; it is warranted free from all mineral or metallic ingredients, or oxide of zinc, of which most Cosmetics are composed, and which ruin the skin. It effectually disperses Chaps, Chilblains, Freckles, Tan, Sunburn, Stings of Insects, Redness, Roughness of the Skin; relieves Irritation of the Skin, Prickly Heat, &c., renders the

SKIN SOFT AND SMOOTH,

and produces a beautiful, pure, and delicate complexion. Size **4s. 6d.** and **8s. 6d.**; half-sized bottles, **2s. 3d.**

ROWLANDS' ESSENCE OF TYRE

Effectually dyes red or grey hair a permanent brown or black. **4s.**

ROWLANDS' EUKONIA.

A pure Toilet Powder in three tints, White, Rose, and Cream, for ladies of a Brunette complexion and those who do not like white powder. Boxes, **1s.**; large boxes, **2s. 6d.**

Ask Chemists for ROWLANDS' ARTICLES, of 20, HATTON GARDEN, LONDON, and avoid spurious imitations.

The Diet of all Lucky Dogs

Copyright.
Spratts Patent Ltd

SPRATTS PATENT
DOG CAKES.